FACING YOUR FEARS:
THE DEVON BERRY STORY

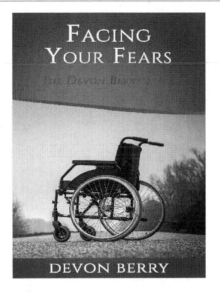

BY DEVON BERRY

Copyright © 2017

Unless otherwise indicated,
all scriptures are quoted from the
King James Version of the Bible.

Note: *This is a real life story; only the names of the people and schools have been changed due to privacy.*

Dedication

First, I give honor to God who is the head of my life.

This book is dedicated to my family and for those that feel hopeless. Family, if it were not for all of you refusing to make excuses for me, I would not be the man I am today.

To my mother, Tonja Grier, who has set the bar for me:

> When I was down and out, you were the one I leaned on for support. If it were not for your taking and giving me a chance to live and be me, I would not be able to see.
>
> Thank you for telling the doctors no and not aborting me. Thank you Mom for teaching me about Christ. Thank you for taking care of me when I was sick in the hospital; you saw me at my lowest point. If it were not for you, my Dad and my siblings, we would not be here today.
>
> I just want to thank you, Mom, for being a great parent and the best Mom. You deserve everything that God has for you, because you stepped up to - and far beyond - the plate for more than people give you credit for. Far too often you had to be the Mom and Dad and I love and thank you for planting the seed of Christ in my life. When I look at you, I see strength and integrity. You are the reason I continue to go on and I just want to thank you and tell you how much I love you dearly.

To my Dad John Berry:

There were a lot of times when we did not see eye to eye, but I want to thank you for teaching me discipline and how to be respectful of others. You did care for my siblings and I when Mom could not and you were there for us when you could be. Even when you weren't, I knew you wanted to be.

Thank you Dad for teaching me Christ and being in my life. I am proud to call you Dad. Thank you for showing me and my siblings Christ.

To My sisters Destinee and Jayana:

You two are the epitome of excellence; I can go on and on about you. You both have stuck up and supported me when no one else would. You two were a huge part of me giving my life to Christ.

Thank you for putting up with me and helping me even when you did not want to. You two beautiful, young ladies represent Christ well and are an example of how a lady should carry and present herself.

You took my walker, you rolled me in my chair, you cooked, you clean, you told me the truth, etc. These are all actions that you showed just because you love and care for me. You love and care for me so much that you both would put your life on the line for me. When no one else was there, you two were. I could not be prouder to be your big brother and I love you both with all my heart.

To My Big brother John Berry Jr.:

Thank you for being the best brother in the world. You showed me how to be tough and you are a true loving and caring brother.

You stuck up for me when others did me wrong; you always had my back. You stepped up and was a big brother to all of us.

You took care of us when our parents were not there. The responsibility and respect you showed was more than just being a great biological brother, but a great friend.

You are amazingly talented in a bevy of ways. Bro, I look up to you in a lot of ways, but nothing beats our bond and the love we have for each other that runs deeper than blood. Nothing can get in the way of us, bro. But the love we have for each other is like none other. We may have fussed and fought, but I would not trade you in for any other brother in the world.

You are the inspiration that motivates me and a huge reason I am the man I am today. Thank you for your support, the smiles I have when I am in your presence and the happiness you bring to my life. I love you forever.

Auntie Jean Turner:

You are like a second mom to me but, more importantly, you taught me Christ. You are an example of a God fearing woman and I thank you for keeping me all those years and still encouraging me each and every day. You and your husband, Uncle Jeff Turner, have played significant roles in my life, encouraging me every time I see you. You both have been there for us when no one else was.

To my Great Auntie Sis (Mrs. Tomlinson) and God Mother Hopey (Mrs. Battle):

Thank you for being so sweet and taking care of me and my siblings all of those years. You two have been wonderful Godmothers to us.

To my Grandad John Robert Berry (Granddaddy Jr.):

Even though you're dead and gone, I think about the times we shared while I was young. I remember telling you that I was going to play football and I did, Grandad, just for you. You were the best Grandad in the world. Rest in Heaven until we meet again.

Thank you to all of you who have helped me along the way. I am sure I left many names out, but I would like to say thank you to everyone who ever contributed to me.

To those who have no hope, remember **Jeremiah 29:11**:

For I know the thoughts that I think towards you, saith the LORD, thoughts and thoughts of peace and not of evil, to give you an expected end.

Luke 1:37: *For with God Nothing Shall Be Impossible.*

1 Corinthians 2:5: *Let your faith not stand in the wisdom of man but in the power of God.*

God loves you and there is hope. Trust in him and remember, there are **no excuses** in life. May God Bless you!

Preface

First, I give Honor to GOD who is the Head of my life. My name is Devon Berry and I want to tell the untold story about my life of Trials and Tribulations.

While reading this book, you will find out:

- what happened to me.

- how everyone picked on me because I was different with different abilities.

- how the devil tried to steal my joy on many occasions and.

- how I was stabbed in the back and used.

- how I dealt with adversity, discrimination and racism.

I was also talked about by family members - while others picked on and taunted me - because I refused to be stereotyped, but was determined to stand out and be different. The doctors said No, but God said YES.

This story is about how a young boy refused to let his disability hinder him from playing football and other sports. It is also a story about how I persevered and refused to be subjected to the bias of society and to take No for an answer.

If I can, so can you. Through these pages you will learn how you can deal with whatever society is throwing at you right now. My keys to victory are putting God first and surrendering my life to Jesus Christ. Our victory is not of man, but a supernatural orchestration by God. With God all things are possible through Christ Jesus.

I hope that my testimony of faith and belief in God will not only inspire you, but will also help you to believe and trust in Him. Doing this will change your life forever. With His help, you will stop making excuses and will face your fears to live a life with no regrets.

-Devon Berry

No more Excuses - the Devon Berry Story.

Table of Contents

Dedication _____ 2

*Preface*_____ 6

Chapter 1: Circumstances of My Birth as a Twin_____ 9

Chapter 2: Life in Kindergarten/ Elementary School ___ 25

Chapter 3: Life in another Elementary School_____ 38

Chapter 4: Balancing School Life and Surgery _____ 47

Chapter 5: Moving Out of the Projects _____ 55

Chapter 6: Taking Hold of Hope and Persevering _____ 60

Chapter 7: Moving Back to the Projects _____ 67

Chapter 8: Life in the 5th Grade _____ 74

Chapter 9: Life in the 6th Grade _____ 83

Chapter 10: Overcoming a Difficult Coach and Playing
Football in the 6th Grade _____ 89

Chapter 11: Life in the 7th Grade _____ 96

Chapter 12: The Discovering New Sports_____ 104

Chapter 13: Life in the 8th Grade _____ 112

Chapter 14: Life in the 9th Grade _____ 118

Chapter 15: Life in the 10th Grade _____ 127

Chapter 16: My Final Year of High School_____ 141

*Conclusion*_____ 150

Chapter 1: Circumstances of My Birth as a Twin

Birthing Premature Twins

My life was hard from the day that I was born and some people doubted my survival from the very beginning. It was a test of faith for all those who were prepared for what would happen to me.

My Mom, **Tonja Grier,** is 5'3 with dark brown eyes and dark skin. She has long, shoulder length black hair with hints of brown and red. She is a heavyset lady who always wears a big smile.

At the time of my birth, she was married to my father, **John Berry Sr**. He is very tall, 6'4, and has dark brown eyes and a dark brown complexion. He too loves to smile and regularly wears a buzz haircut.

What an amazing miracle: two babies ready to enter into the world. My Mom had the usual expectations of hearing her babies' first cries and screams after giving birth. But life often delivers strange twists and surprises.

December 17, 1996 was the day that my twin sister - Destinee Berry- and I were born 2 ½ months premature! This was a nightmare for any family and mother, having to give birth to twins who were not fully developed.

Our initial birthday was February 1997 but, during an ultrasound, the doctors warned my parents that our births would carry complications. The doctors did not know which one of us would have a problem, but they knew that our birth could be life threatening. Their suggestion, or best medical advice, was for my mother to have an abortion.

My mother said that *the pressure of losing a child through abortion was like asking someone to go to hell.* She told me that she chose not to have an abortion because of her faith in God. She was not going to abort us and decided that no matter what, she was going to be there for us as long as she lived. As a result, my Mom was very sick while pregnant with me and my twin sister.

Life Threatening Complications

During the premature birth process, I was the first to arrive. I was coming out so quickly that my Mom called for help because she knew that something was wrong.

The doctors jumped to action, but pulled my head the wrong way in the process, inducing a stroke. Immediately after my arrival, they rushed me to another room, where they hooked me up to multiple cords, an oxygen tank and placed me on *life support*.

According to my Mom, she was in excruciating pain and screamed with tears running down her face like Usain Bolt running the 100m Dash. After about 30 minutes, the doctors put my Mom on a heavy dose of medication to numb the pain from my birth.

To further complicate things, my sister Destinee began to kick in my Mom's stomach as if she was trying to kick a wall of steel. Her position in the birth canal would result in a breached birth, so the doctors decided to perform a C-section because she was on the verge of death.

Although her twins were on the verge of death and fighting for their lives, my Mom was able to live with a clean conscience of not aborting us. Despite her immense physical pain and weakness, my Mom said that she stayed with us as long as she could and made up in her mind that she would stay with us for as long as she was alive.

God was with us to the end and we survived. We were considered to be miracle babies in many people's eyes. I just say it is the favor of God upon us because He showed mercy to us. But the fight was a long way from being over.

[11]

A Fight to Live

My Mom had to stay with us for about two to three months because we were so sick. I suffered from multiple breathing problems and my twin sister had heart problems. We both had to wear heart monitors due to our low heart rates. Imagine babies who were only two pounds and a few ounces suffering from problems so severe.

According to my Mom, we were so small and fragile that **both of us could fit in one of her hands!** We had extreme fevers that would sky rocket; I personally had countless seizures and threw up EVERYWHERE. I had gastric reflux and threw up every time I consumed liquids or solid food.

My twin sister and I were eventually able to eat, but only through a feeding tube. We were so sick that we could not breast feed, so we had to *eat the fat off my Mom's thigh and back.* This might sound unusual, but it was how life was for us at that time and we had to *suffer through it.*

I can only imagine what my Mom went through while facing the possibility of her twins' death. I imagine how she struggled with feelings of hopelessness, bitterness, doubt and depression.

To make matters worse, the house we lived in was run down and roach infested. Nevertheless, it was the place we called home.

The house was owned by Mr. Underwood: a very nice, but elderly man. Mr. Underwood was of an average height and had blue eyes and white hair that looked like wool. He made sure we were always safe.

While growing up, I remained very sick but Destinee

became healthy. My older brother John, named after my Dad and nicknamed *Jay*, watched us when my parents could not. Jay, who is 1 year and 10 months older than me, is average height, dark skinned, very slim and has dark brown eyes.

The Tough Years of Early Childhood

After we were born, life became very hard for my family. My twin sister Destinee and I were carried in incubators because we still had heart monitors and were so small. To give up a visual perspective, both of us fit in one car seat and had to wear baby doll clothing.

Our survival was a day-to-day process. I had to be fed through a feeding tube that was connected to the side of my lower abdomen. I had constant seizures so I needed to be in a safe environment where I could be monitored closely.

I could not go to a regular daycare to the severity of my condition. I eventually attended preschool at *McDonough Primary*. When I was about 3 years old, I was placed in the Special Education room, which was very stressful for me.

Life at home was also very stressful and I remember my Mom and Dad having heated discussions. Sometimes the discussions were so heated that it led to abuse and the police being called to our home.

Since the time that I was a year old, my Mom wondered if I would ever be able to walk. When I was 3 years old, my Mom took me to the hospital to see if something was wrong with my legs. I was officially diagnosed with **cerebral palsy**.

Cerebral palsy is a condition that affects a person mentally and physically. In my case, by the grace of God, it was only slightly physical, affecting the left side of my brain that controls motor skills like walking and writing.

From early on, I would always try to walk but could not and did not understand why. As a result, life as a young child was very hard for me.

My First Surgery

As a family, we always had to struggled financially, including very little food to eat to wondering where we would sleep. Adding to the struggle was the fact that my parents had four children, after the birth of my younger sister **Jayanna**. Having one child was hard enough to deal with, but my parents had four including one with a disability.

My first surgery occurred when I was 4 years old, under the guidance of orthopedic surgeon **Dr. Schmitt**. He recommended that I have surgery to try to straighten my feet and ankles. The whole family was in fear of what the outcome was going to be.

According to my Mom, the doctors informed her that the surgery included cutting the side of my ankles and Achilles heel. As a Christian family, we went immediately into fervent prayer.

Our church, which we still attend, is an old fashion, Pentecostal church in McDonough, Georgia. Back then it was pastored by Bishop Herman Barber (now deceased). He was an elderly man of average height, with grey hair, fairly brown skin and a humped back. My Mom took me to the front of the church to receive prayers concerning my upcoming surgery.

Since we were born, my Mom sought prayers for my twin sister and I. Bishop Barber laid hands on me and prayed to God that all would go well during my surgery. The biggest fear we faced was whether I would survive the surgery.

Prayer Support from Our Church

Church life was all I knew since I was born and raised in the church. We stayed in church almost 24/7, so I knew in my heart that surgery would not be a problem. I draw my encouragement from prophet Isaiah:

"Thus saith the LORD unto you, Be not afraid nor dismayed by reason of this great multitude; for the battle is not yours, but God's."

2 Chronicles 20:15

Going into the surgery, I never asked my Mom, *Why me?* My youth allowed me to be oblivious to how serious this way, but not to the fear I saw in my parents' eyes. I was completely silent on my way to the hospital, but I could hear my Mom praying for a sense of hope and the grace to keep the faith.

Trusting God at an Early Age

As for me, at the tender age of 4, the following scripture was going through my mind:

"God resisteth the proud, but giveth grace unto the humble."

James 4:6

In the hope that things would go well, my Mom and I prayed to GOD before getting out of the car at Egleston Child Health Care of Atlanta. We prayed again as we were at the entrance of the hospital:

"GOD, thank You that I can do all things through Christ who strengthens me."

Philippians 4:13

As we entered the elevator on our way to the waiting room, I remember seeing a baby that seemed to have had brain surgery. Her skull was cut four ways and you could see the scars on her forehead. We learned that she had also had heart surgery, which explained the fear in the eyes of her parents. I started thinking about how my surgery could be just as a bad or even worse than hers.

I turned my head away; seeing their pain made my skin crawl. As we got off the elevator, my Mom looked at me and said, "Son, just know that I love you with all my heart." I replied, "GOD is going to come in with me into the surgery and back out with me."

As I laid down on the cart and waited on the nurse to give me a gown, I began to think about the possibilities of losing my life. I was scared. At only 4 years old, I did not quite understand why all of this stuff was going on or why I needed all of these things to be done to me. All I knew was they were trying to cut my legs open.

My Mom told me that the surgery was to help straighten out my legs because they were weak and I was duck-footed. She told me that it was important for me to realize that this was a life or death situation.

The nurse arrived with a needle; she stuck me in my arm and wrapped a tape around it. I asked her, "What is this and why does is it hurt so bad?" She told me it was to take my blood and make sure my levels were okay.

I did not understand; all I knew was that it was very painful. As time went by, I saw scrapes on the side of the hospital bed and I started saying, "I got to go." I remember seeing about 20 doctors in the room and I wondered, *GOD why me?*

The doctors gave me some medicine to knock me out and I was afraid that I was not going to wake back up. I dozed off and saw a bright light over me. In the light, I saw someone that looked like an angel. He said to me, "*Fear not for I am an Angel of the Lord and through His stripes you are healed. You are going make it so have no worries.*" He also quoted **Isaiah 41:10**:

> *"Fear thou not; for I am with thee: be not dismayed; for I am GOD I will strengthen thee; yea, I will help thee; yea I will uphold thee with the right hand of my righteousness."*

From that point on, I knew that I was special. I knew that there was something different about me. After a long while, I eventually woke up and they told me I had to be resuscitated during surgery. When I was fully awake, I immediately looked at my legs and was greeted by a sharp pain that took a toll on my whole body.

[19]

As I picked my head up, I saw my Mom on my right side, my Auntie on my left side and in front of me was pain. I screamed for help and my Mom and Auntie immediately got hold of me as the tears rolled down my face like a flood.

4 Years Old and My First Thought of Suicide

After the surgery, all I could think of was how much pain I would have to endure, until an amazing thing happened.

The moment I cried, **"JESUS"**, a voice said, **"Don't worry."** Unfortunately, there was another voice telling me, *"You are worthless."*

I was thinking about the pain and, on the inside, I felt empty and hopeless. I looked up and said, *"JESUS, do you know what You are doing?"* (Remember, I was only 4 years old at this time.)

My Auntie Jean said, "Son, all is well." She is a woman of strong faith and always said to me, *"Keep the faith and do not lose sight of the truth that God is going to heal you one day."* She told me that one day I would walk.

The nurse arrived and asked if everything was okay. My Mom said yes, but I said NO! I couldn't take the pain anymore and needed more pain medication. I cried for at least five hours straight because the pain was so intense.

There were many days when I did not eat anything and I grew weak physically and mentally. I felt like I was done with life because it *sucked so bad* and I wanted to kill myself. However, I kept the faith and eventually ate something.

I was very quiet because I was in so much mental anguish at the time. My Mom cried but she was happy that there were no complications and I did not die during surgery.

Days went by and I was finally released from the hospital. My Dad, sisters and my brother called me at the hospital before I was released, which made me feel a little bit better.

The cast on my legs were blue and went all the way up to my thighs. There was also a long bar that connected my ankles. The ride home was very rough and I was not only tired, but felt weak as I cried the whole way home.

I discovered that I had more dead skin on my legs than a dead person's body, so life was hard for me. When I got home, my brothers and sisters rushed out of the house to hug me. To their surprise, I was sound asleep. My Mom gave me something to ease the pain on the way home.

When I woke up, my brother Jay was crying and talking about how he missed me. My sisters were crying too, *tears of joy* they said. I enjoyed all the attention and affections but, more importantly, the fact that I did not have to do anything in the house. (I was only four years old, mind you.)

Homeschooled for 10 Weeks

I was not allowed to go back to school for 10 weeks. This was tough on me because my brother and sisters had to go to school, my parents had to go to work and I had to go to my Auntie's house. Don't get me wrong, I loved my Auntie but I missed my parents and siblings.

Auntie took good care of me and she sure could cook! My Aunt has brown eyes and was about 5 ft. tall. The surgery meant that I would miss 10 weeks of school and had to be homeschooled. During these times, I did a lot of praying and seeking God for help.

The teacher that homeschooled me was Mrs. Prittchet. She was an elderly lady – slender, about 5' 8 and had green or blue eyes. She was a very nice lady and always pushed me to do better and to never give up. She worked with me on my ABC's and counting.

I was a little bit slow to comprehend initially but, eventually, I grasped what she was teaching me. There were days and nights when I said to myself, *I cannot do this* and I would ball over and cry like it was my last day on earth. At the end, I always said to myself, *I am going to make it; I am going to get through this.*

During those 10 weeks, I had to get lots of physical therapy and treatments. I remember saying, "It hurts; I cannot do this. It hurts Momma, why me?" She would say, "They are trying to get your legs stronger."

They were testing me out with leg braces, walkers and crutches because they knew that I was going to need support to walk. With my fifth birthday closely approaching, I had to get tested for additional things.

I also had to have a follow-up appointment with my orthopedic surgeon, Dr. Schmitt. The checkup went okay, but he said that there was a huge possibility of me having another surgery. The prognosis was that my legs were still bent so another corrective surgery was recommended.

If that was not scary enough, they were discussing the possibility of cutting me close to my private area and my ankles to help straighten my legs. As a result, I became very depressed but I knew that God was going to bring me through it.

Chapter 2: Life in Kindergarten/ Elementary School

Disability and Public School Life

My fifth birthday finally came and it was a bitter sweet time for me. The thought of another surgery was just too scary for me to have any fun. I was still in physical therapy and they did an MRI to test my motor skills and found some problems.

I eventually enrolled back in an elementary and kindergarten school. My teacher was Mrs. Turtle; she had a slender built, loved to smile and always wore glasses over her blue eyes. (I think she was on the verge of retirement.)

School was a bit challenging for me and I always struggled to comprehend things and to punctuate my writing. Kids laughed and picked on me and would say to me, "Hey crippled monkey." They also called me ugly while saying that they were better than me because they could walk and run. They said things like:

- "I wish you would die, you crippled SOB, stupid mother…"

- "You are a Special Education student; why can't you walk?"

- "Your legs are not straight" (and they would call me everything else under the sun).

Eventually, the school placed me in the self-contained Special Education room and I felt that it was a discrimination against me. I felt humiliated because I was different and I still could not understand why all of these things happened to me. Sometimes, while I was alone (which was a lot of times), I say to myself, *I thought all men were created equal?*

I cried to my parents saying that I was just a person that wanted to fit in. I used to always tell people that I was born this way. On the inside, I was very insecure because of what I was going through but, on the outside, I was a very bright and happy-go-lucky person that loved God. Life in the classroom was very hard for me because I was always picked on for my disability.

As a result, I was mad at the world but later discovered that what I was going through was God's plan for me. Before this realization, I was spitting on my teachers or scratching and punching kids because they made fun of me for no reason (or so I thought). Every time I was placed in the Special Education room, I always said to myself, *One day you are going to make it out of this place. One day, it will not be the same because you are going to change the game.*

I knew that I had an ambitious mindset and I believed the following words of Martin Luther King, Jr.:

> *The ultimate measure of a man is not where he stands in moments of comfort and convenience, but where he stands at times of challenge and controversy.*

I also heeded the advice to *put your faith in Him (Jesus)*. From the moment I received the revelation of these sayings, my faith began to come into effect. Nevertheless, simultaneously, the devil was still trying to steal, kill and destroy my life.

Life at Home with Dad

As time was getting closer to my second surgery, life at home was taking its toll. We moved at least three times in one year and living with my family had its ups and downs.

My Mom was gone a lot because she was going to college which left my Dad to watch and take care of us. Most of the time, my Dad was nice but, when you made him angry, it was a wrap. I sometimes received beatings for no reason. My Dad and I had a lot of disagreements and we still do to this day.

My Dad was particularly strict on me. When I did something wrong, he would kick to punish me; he would slam, kick or beat me with switches or belt buckles. There was one particular incident where he choked me. Sometimes, he beat me for no apparent reason or because I had to use the restroom.

My Mom, on the other hand, was more protective of me but, at times, she would drag us by our shirts while beating us with brooms and switches. Despite my parents' abusive moments, we always went to church and I always preached about the man called Nicodemus (**John 3:4-8**):

> "How can someone be born when they are old?" Nicodemus asked. "Surely they cannot enter a second time into their mother's womb to be born!" 5 Jesus answered, "Very truly I tell you, no one can enter the kingdom of God unless they are born of water and the Spirit. 6 Flesh gives birth to flesh, but the Spirit gives birth to spirit. 7 You should not be surprised at my saying, 'You must be born again.' 8 The wind blows wherever it pleases. You hear its sound, but you cannot tell where it comes from or where it is going. So it is with everyone born of the Spirit."

At our church, I was always asked to preach a sermon because many of the members believed I was a *Living Testimony* and knew the above verses were my favorite to preach. Often, my Aunt Jean and others - such as the deacons, elders and Bishop Barber - would lay hands on me and encourage me to keep the faith. They would also say that one day, I would walk and all was well with me.

Time for My Second Surgery

Time passed and, before I knew it, it was time for another surgery. I never liked surgeries nor saw the point of them. All I knew was that I was going to go through more pain and suffering.

Going into my second surgery, I did not know what to expect but I knew one thing for sure: GOD was going to have my back, lead me and guide me in the right path as He said in **Isaiah 41:10**:

> *"So do not fear, for I am with you; do not be dismayed, for I am your God. I will strengthen you and help you; I will uphold you with my righteous right hand."*

> ### Isaiah 41:13:

> *"For I am the LORD your God who takes hold of your right hand and says to you, Do not fear; I will help you."*

I also knew that I had to wear the whole amour of GOD and walk according to **James 4:7**:

> *"Submit yourselves, then, to God. Resist the devil, and he will flee from you."*

In faith, I took these verses everywhere I went as I kept them in my heart. Although I was only five years old, I knew that GOD was with me. I believed His promise that *those who desire His Word and are thirsty for it, will receive His Word, knowledge and truth and understanding.*

As we prepared for surgery, I prayed: *Lord, please bless this word.* Surgery was another test of faith because I always had this fear that I might never have the ability to stand on my own and might die from the procedure.

Nevertheless, I had to walk in faith because **Hebrews 11:6** tells us:

> "And without faith it is impossible to please God, because anyone who comes to him must believe that he exists and that he rewards those who earnestly seek him."

As a result of my faith in GOD, I was determined to trust Him. I told my Mom that GOD was going with me in and out of the surgery. Also, right before the surgery, I prayed to GOD and asked Him to cover me in His blood and to protect and guide me through it all. Then, I recalled that "by His stripes ye are healed" (**Isaiah 53:5**).

As I opened my eyes after prayer, I saw that there were doctors gathered around me and angels around me as well. They were saying the Lord's Prayer in **Matthew 6:9-13:**

> "Our Father which art in heaven, Hallowed be thy name. 10 Thy kingdom come. Thy will be done in earth, as it is in heaven. 11 Give us this day our daily bread. 12 And forgive us our debts, as we forgive our debtors. 13 And lead us not into temptation, but deliver us from evil: For thine is the kingdom, and the power, and the glory, forever. Amen."
>
> [LORD, please bless this word.]

I was eventually knocked out by the medication in my IV. When I woke up and opened my eyes, I saw that there were ice packs around my neck and I saw the heart rate monitor zigzag and then flat line. It got to the point that they had to resuscitate me.

I can tell that the devil was happy in his attempt to take my life but I said, "I rebuke the devil in the name of JESUS." Immediately, the heart monitor went from low to high! I finally fell asleep at about 1 pm and did not wake up until 8 pm. When I woke, the pain was excruciating but I wore a smile on my face because I knew that GOD brought me through the surgery. I knew once again that I was special because God gave me a vision that I was going to be unique.

I now faced another battle: the realization that I had to go home at some point. I didn't know how to handle it so I used what was familiar. I read basic biblical stories in an effort to increase my strength and power. Once again I was suicidal because I felt there was no other way out of my situation. Life was simply too hard.

I began to think about the struggles at home with my Dad - from the way he treated me and my Mom. I started to think about the challenges of my life, especially my disability. It was my Mom who helped me keep my faith in God.

I continued to study the Word of God and was encouraged by **Philippians 4:13**:

> "I can do all things through Christ which strengtheneth me."

I also believed the Word of God in **Luke 1:37**:

> "For with God nothing shall be impossible."

Eventually, I got better and the doctors told my Mom that it was ok for me to go home and I was stable enough to be on my own. They recommended monthly follow up appointments with a pediatrician. As a result, I had to make countless trips to the doctor's office and undergo numerous hours of therapy. I also had to go to a chiropractor.

There were times that I did not want to do any of it, but I did because I knew it would be beneficial to everyone in the long run. However, as I got physically stronger, life at home was getting worst. As always, I kept my faith in GOD.

Although the struggles in my body and at home were real, they made me a stronger person. Through the struggles, I learned not to be afraid of adversities and tribulations.

There were a lot of decisions to be made and some of them were life lessons while others were pointless. I could have easily thrown in the towel, but I refused to give up because I knew I was special. This knowledge helped me make it through as people talked about me and made fun of me. I knew that if I could 'talk the talk' and 'walk the walk', they could not harm me.

GOD said to me, "Be still" and I did just that. At times, I felt messed up and confused, but I let GOD know that I trusted Him. I kept the faith.

The Motivators along the Way

I chose not to criticize the people that talked about me and not to give up on myself. Most importantly, I chose not to give up on God and my family because I knew that a time was coming when I was going to be happy.

There were many times when I just wanted to throw in the towel and say, "I'm done with this; I can't do it anymore." Instead, I chose to face reality and accept that I had to press through. Although what was happening to me was very bad, I realized that no one was going to feel sorry for me; I had to confront my situation. Being second class was no easy feat, especially as a young black, disabled male.

Eventually, I went back to Elementary School. My teacher was Mrs. Gilreth. Mrs. Gilreth had green eyes, brown hair and a very soft voice that was calm and relaxing. Sometimes she just let us draw, color and play around.

I can remember my first grade teacher, Jake, who asked me, "What is wrong with you?" I told him that "I was born this way." He said, "But your legs are not moving." I said, "Yes, they are in Malaysia this week and I have this thing called cerebral palsy." (I could not say the name of my condition correctly so the teacher said it for me.) I struggled in that class to learn my ABCs and with my handwriting.

I remember my kindergarten teacher who repeatedly told me that my handwriting was not the best and that I jumbled up my words. She said, "Honey, your words don't have to be so jumbled up together." I had no idea what she was talking about, but I knew that she was trying to help me.

I had to go to tutoring and to speech classes to learn how to speak correctly. I also had to go to handwriting classes because I could not write properly. My teacher would review my classwork with me and tell me not to worry about things. She said that I should not let the things I worry about get in the way of my tomorrow. "I'm here to help you", she told me, but it was a psychological struggle for me because I could not understand the class work.

One day, my Mom said, "Son, you got to go take the Moron Test because you're stuck." I began to practice and improved much due to repetition. I was finally beginning to learn that the teacher was correct in thinking that I was a moron, but I refused to just sit there for 30 minutes and do nothing. From then on, I tried to get better and my progress began when I started listening to her. I finally wrote a paper and she gave me a foreword to it.

I can still remember the smile on my face and the hard work that I had put in. I said to myself, "I love you very much" and patted my own back because I knew that there were greater things for me to achieve.

My teacher told me to stop looking for a way to tap out and I told her that I could not stop trying self-improvement. She said, "You are going to keep grinding and don't stop because you know reality sets in if you don't pass your quiz or test." From that point on, everything mattered to me.

I decided that I would give 100% and not stop because I wanted to be successful. I can remember Mrs. Gilreth asking me, "What do you want to be when you grow up?" I said, "I want to be a preacher and motivator." She said, "You can definitely be a motivator."

I had my first flip side episode as I was going into class and thought about needing another surgery to connect my legs all the way up to my hip. I also knew that it would cause a financial burden on my family, which was very hard for me.

I had not talked about it but, when people limited me, I flipped on them saying, "You cannot do what you are doing to me because I am a good person." For a long time, I had to pretend I was okay as people were saying things to me that were cruel, but not this time.

When I spoke to my Mom about it, she said, "You're just going to have to learn that everybody's not going to be in your corner. You will always hear things from them." I heard and experienced it firsthand with some of my family members, because they were always trying to 'second class' me.

My Third Desire to Commit Suicide

The one question that I always asked was, "Why me? Why do I have to go through these things?" My Mom said, "What you're going to have to do is keep trusting God and keep the Faith."

At the time, I did not understand what she meant because I was only five or six years old. Now I realize that she meant I would have to confront things mentally, physically and emotionally; everything! When Mom discovered that I was thinking about suicide, she said, "That's not the way of the Lord." She explained to me saying, "If you kill yourself, then you're going to die and you will go to hell because I cannot come get you."

After she said these things to me, I got kind of scared. Mom was always telling me about Adam and Eve and how God could not have given me this great miracle without being a Christian. From that day forward, I knew that I did not have to buy more things, but needed to keep my eyes on the Bible. With my Dad providing food to my Mom and us, we were ok.

As a result, I would look into my Bible, get a verse and take it to school. Sometime, right there in the self-contained classroom, I would remember a Bible verse so that I did not have to deal with all the hatred and prejudice that I had to go through. It was hard to be in the self-contained classroom, but I graduated from first grade.

I said to Mom, "You know what? I passed." She had great tears in her eyes and I said, "Why you crying?" She said, "You have overcome so much."

I did not know what to do when I passed the first grade,

but I was so very happy about it. My Mom held me very tight and so did my Dad when he found out that I passed. (Remember I started out in Special Education.)

My Mom said, "You have a testimony to tell" and I was like, "What exactly are you talking about? What is a testimony?" Now I know.

In the meantime, you - the reader of this book - will always have testimonies so I would like you to contact me when you have one. I am not the type to get scared anytime someone has a testimony.

Chapter 3: Life in another Elementary School

We Move to Jackson, Georgia

We moved to a place in Butts County called Jackson, Georgia and some of the kids there were nice while others were mean. When I told my Mom about it, she said, "Don't retaliate because, if you do, they don't care and they really don't want you there." So, I said, "I can't do this but I know that ultimately, God will bring me through." Why would He let my Mom move us to Jackson so that my teacher can look at me and say, "Maybe, maybe you are smart?"

At that moment, I said to myself, "I am smart because I am a child of God." I also realized that there is no stopping me because I know that the anointing of God is on me.

When I moved down there, the kids did not accept me. Most intelligent people did not like me, but I made up my mind to be comfortable. There was little to do in Jackson and all the students wanted to play basketball, football, run track and occasionally wrestle.

When you have a lot of people that are very nice, there will also be some that are judgmental. They give you long looks and ask a lot of questions. I was not the type of person that would reject anyone's question, but moving to Jackson made me realize that I was considered the minority. I began to ask myself, "How shall I overcome this stereotype?"

I made up my mind to have a reality check by not only recognizing my fears, but facing them head on. I did this knowing that on a personal level, we are judged as to whether we are *lawfully* right, not whether we are *morally* right.

I always ask myself, "Why do we judge people for who they are?" I never understood the answer to this question or why people judge someone for the color of his or her skin.

As time went by, I got used to living in rural Jackson. It is a very small place but has great food and, although some were very judgmental, many were welcoming.

Attending Elementary School in Jackson

Jackson Elementary, the school my Dad graduated from, was a Title 1 School that did not have a lot of amenities. The lights in the school were dimmed and it was very old. It was here that I met my first friend, Daquarius Wise, who we called DQ.

DQ was 4' 6 with brown skin, brown eyes and he loved to laugh. We made a connection over sports and talked about sports and girls in general. The most interesting thing about us was our favorite food - chicken. (I loved me some chicken!) I was always the one to tell him to get back on track.

As time went on, I began to gain more friends, but some of the students looked at me as a kid that was trying his best to be normal. Some asked me what was wrong with me and I told them that God wanted me to be the way I was. They would laugh and make fun of me. Sometimes I cried, but my Mom told me not to worry about them because some people were mean and everyone was not going to be my friend. She told me that I just had to *live with it*. I guess she was right; as the year went on, I made more friends regardless of the negative students.

During this time, my teacher repeatedly told me, "You don't write well." I said, "Well, it is because of my motor skills." I went on to say, "I can't help it; it is because of my disability called cerebral palsy." I also said that cerebral refers to the brain and palsy refers to physical. I explained how, at birth, I had a stroke which caused complications that affected my handwriting, ability to walk, lack of strength in my hands and, in some cases, pronunciations of my words.

Placed Again in a Special Ed Class

My teacher told me to work on my ABC's. As class went on, I began to realize that they were taking me out of class into a smaller group. I was the type of kid that always asked questions. I was assigned to a 'Parapro' (Paraprofessional Educator) and his name was Mr. Tingle.

Mr. Tingle was Caucasian with blue eyes, brown hair and was about 5'10. He loved to smile and was very cool. I asked him, "Why I can't I stay in the classroom with the other kids?" He replied, "This group right here (my group) needs extra time on their work and they finish their work slower."

Being the curious person that I am, I replied, "What does it matter as long as we get our work done?" Mr. Tingle replied, "We are giving you time and opportunity to finish your work at your pace." I said it was fine by me as long as I got to finish my work.

When I told my parents about it, they said that it was because I was a little slower than the other kids. I said to myself:

I thought this was a country of equality?

Why do they take me out?

Is it because of my disability?

Is it because I am black or is it because I am different?

I prayed to GOD and asked Him why they were treating me differently. GOD revealed to me that I was a 'peculiar child' and that it was who I was as a person. At first, I struggled with what He said, immediately denying the fact that I was different, but accepting who I was and *whose*

I was.

At this time, I had a closed mind; I was very upset and not willing to accept the reality of my life for what it was. I mean, I would say, "Lord, why me? Why are you letting me go through these horrific things?" My Mom tried her best to make things better.

Mom: "Son, it's alright; don't be upset."

Me: "Why do they separate me? Why do they treat me differently at school?"

Parents: "It is just how the world is; it is not your friend. It does not care about your feelings or that you are different."

"Son, this is just an ugly world."

Me: "But why?"

Refusing to Face My Condition

I did not quite understand what my parents were saying to me, because I did not understand that being in a special group would actually help me. I was still stuck on the fact that they were treating me differently rather than realizing that I had a learning disability.

Also, I did not understand the difference between racism and equality. I am who I am and I could either accept it or choose to be ignorant. I can choose to dwell in self-pity, to be very arrogant, stubborn and refuse to face reality. These were sources of my insecurity; I was blind and refused to face my reality. Only God helped me to find **James 4:6-7**:

> *"But he giveth more grace wherefore he saith, God resisteth the proud but giveth grace unto the humble. 7 Submit yourselves to GOD resist the devil, and he will flee from you."*

I came to realize that Mr. Tingle was not trying to be mean to me, but he recognized that I had different abilities and needed help. Once I received that revelation, I accepted that I needed extra time on my work and began to accept who I was. As the year progressed, I continued to receive tutoring and I just 'grinded it out' (studied hard) no matter what. I did not understand every test, every worksheet and every project, but I always tried my hardest.

During that time, I was placed on an IEP (Individual Education Plan) designed for kids like myself. An IEP is for kids with different abilities that vary between learning how to write to needing extra time for assignments. In other words, it is a program for kids who need extra help or have special needs.

For example, I needed extra time on my work and I needed

a copy of all assignments or notes from class. I also needed to take home every book from all my classes. I was assigned a 'Parapro' in each. In addition to this, I needed a special desk made just for me and I used it to my full advantage.

Realizing the fact that I was very intellectual, I decided to utilize my IEP to the fullest potential. As a result, my teachers saw huge improvements in my test scores and work assignments. My handwriting was still not the best, but there was an improvement from the beginning of the year to the end. Nevertheless, I was proud that I made a huge improvement, but I was still dealing with emotional and mental issues of why the kids at school still picked on me.

Every time the kids picked on me, I would get upset, throw temper tantrums and cry until my teachers realized what the kids were doing. Sometimes, I would ignore them; other times I would retaliate, especially when they said things like, "Hey crazy legs Devon, spider legs, crippled legs, etc." In the heat of my anger I didn't realize that they just wanted to see my reaction so that they could laugh at me.

Overcoming Rebellion

Hitting people every time they said something rude to me resulted in several altercations where I was written up. The Principal, Mrs. Hildebrandt, removed me from the classroom and took me to ISS (In-school Suspension).

The ISS teacher, Mrs. Henderson, was very strict. She asked me why I was in her class and I ignored her. When she asked again, I rudely responded, "I punched someone in the face." She replied, "You did what?" I said again, "I punched someone in the face." Right after I said that, my Auntie Pat walked into ISS room to talk to Mrs. Henderson. Auntie Pat, also a school custodian there, immediately slapped me across the head a few times and cursed me out.

Seeing her, I was determined from that point forward to not get into any more trouble. I guess you could say that *I had learned my lesson.* I went back into the classroom and apologized for what I had done, but the kids continued to pick on me. From that point forward, I ignored them and concentrated on my class work.

I Adopted a PDIG Attitude

After being released from the ISS room, I began to tell myself that I wanted to succeed in life and I was going to be somebody. I did not want to be *a nobody* in life. Of course, I had doubters and naysayers, but I focused on my studies. I said to myself, *Since people doubt me, I will adopt a PDIG attitude.*

PDIG stands for *People Doubting and I Grind* (a determination to study hard). As the year went by, I continued to *grind*, sometimes until 3am or without any sleep at all. I had a strong desire to improve my learning skills against all odds. I give GOD all the praise for helping me strengthen my resolve and determination.

Mind you, that at this time, I was only 8 years old and in the 2nd grade, but that did not stop me from acknowledging God for who He is and where He brought me from. Also, life at home was not always peaches and cream; I was having to deal with the bad relationship and arguments between my parents. Sometimes it led to a physical altercation and my siblings and I had to live under the bad conditions. We all have reason to give God the glory for allowing us to make it through.

During the 2nd grade I said, "God, I will not let anything stop me from being my best because I cannot - and I will not - be stopped." I am here to tell you that during this time in my life, there were a lot of ups and downs, but I still yielded myself to GOD and to God be the Glory.

Chapter 4: Balancing School Life and Surgery

Being a Part of a Baseball Team

I ended up playing for the *Sunshine* in the 2nd Grade. The Sunshine was a leading baseball team and my coach was a cool Caucasian male. The team was originally called White Sox and the name later changed to Warriors. I enjoyed playing T-ball, but did not like the fact that every game we play ended in a tie.

Playing every position helped me stay motivated. In the twists and turns known as my life, I would soon need a source of motivation.

As I was getting ready to go to the 3rd grade, Dr. Schmitt (a pediatrician) informed my Mom and that I needed to have another surgery! According to him, the surgery would assist my development because the doctors would drain fluids out of my knees and move the bones down to my ankles. Again, the doctors told my Mom that there was a possibility that I might die because of my past surgeries, but I told my Mom to keep the faith.

Life in the 3rd Grade

After the summer, I returned to school and my 3rd grade teacher was Mrs. Brown. Mrs. Brown had dark brown eyes, red hair and was very nice.

I always prayed and asked God for strength and favor while in school. I was the kid that always sat in the front of class because the front row allowed me to stay focused on the lesson which helped me to learn better. I still struggled with my spellings, multiplication and comprehension, but I tried my best. My other teacher, Mrs. Jones, always asked me questions because she knew that I was smart. As time passed, I began to get a better understanding of the class work.

The Effects of Being Mocked

Meanwhile, the other 3rd grade kids were often picking on me because I was different. They never understood the pain and suffering they put me through so I started to isolate myself. I needed to be by myself. When I was confronted with the insults from the other kids, I would pray to God for strength and courage because I needed His help.

We always had P.E. (Physical Education) on Fridays and the coaches were Coach K and Coach J. The class was very goofy and fun. Although I was often picked on, they made me feel accepted. They enjoyed having me in the class and I had some good memories of the coaches.

I also had plenty of fond memories with other teachers:

- Chorus teacher Mrs. McMahon. Mrs. McMahon loved my singing and I loved singing for her because when I sing I feel happy. When I sing, I feel like everyone else.

- Art teacher Mr. Bell. In his Art class, I would draw pictures of my emotions and reality. Mr. Bell kept telling me to believe in myself and my dreams.

- Mrs. Jones. Mrs. Jones loved me because I always tried my best. I often struggled while taking a test and she would always help me to understand the test materials. Mrs. Jones kept helping me because she hated to see kids struggle with comprehension of test materials and I accepted her help because I needed it.

We often went to recess and the kids would pick on me but I did not care. The kids made fun of me and they kept laughing at my disability, but I refused to let them bring me down and I refused to let them hinder my development.

After a while, I started getting into more and more trouble. By the end of the year, I ran over the Principal - Mrs. Hildebrand - with my walker or wheelchair! She walked to her office and told me to follow her. I watched as she called my mother and told her that I was using my walker as a physical weapon. My mother was angry about my actions and demanded that I act better or else. I was often disciplined by my Mom and Dad that year, but I eventually got my act together. I started behaving a little better.

My Third Surgery

Meanwhile, the time was getting closer and closer to the next surgery and everyone was getting very emotional. On November 20, 2006 the time had come and I was terrified.

My Mom was scared because of the circumstances and I was very scared to have another surgery. I knew I would have to be homeschooled for the rest of the year and my Auntie Mariam would have to take care of me while my brothers and sisters went to school.

As the doctors were preparing for the surgery and the IV needle was being inserted into my arm, I told my Mom that God was going in and out of the operating room with me. I placed my faith in Him as stated in 1 Corinthians 2:5:

> *"That your faith should not stand in the wisdom of men, but in the power of God."*

I immediately started thanking God for all that He had done for me. When they strapped me down, I reacted frantically. As a result, they had to put me to sleep.

During the surgery, I knew that God was with me and that He was watching over me. I believe that He refused to let me die during that surgery because He saw that I had already been through so much pain and suffering. He did not want it all to be in vain and He loves me.

I received numerous gifts from my family members as well as visits and cards from my classmates. The cards were telling me to, *Get Well Soon*. They made me feel a little better because they showed me that my family and classmates cared about me.

Although my heart was feeling a little warmer, tears were streaming down my face, because I did not understand why I was going through so much pain and suffering. Nevertheless, I persevered.

I trusted in God's plan and purpose for me and kept the faith. Even when I was in so much pain, I perked up whenever my siblings called to check on me; I loved to hear from them. I was also very upset, hurt and disappointed at the turn of events in my life yet again, but I never stopped praying to God.

Living in Pain and Hopelessness

The doctors finally released me from the hospital and I fell asleep on the long drive home. I longed to accomplish my dreams and not be stopped, so I wanted the pain and additional surgeries to come to an end.

We moved into one of the Brown Lee Road townhomes. It was very hard for me to be the only one in the house, especially since I could not get out of bed. Having my Auntie change my diapers made me begin to feel sorry for myself, but playing Madden on PlayStation 2 brought some joy to my life. It made me feel that I was doing something fun; all those countless hours of running touchdowns and sacks. The best part was running back a punt football and the field goals that led to the sweet taste of victory!

I often had to take meds to ease the pain, but some pain never went away. The physical pain was a reminder of my hopeless condition and I hated feeling hopeless. I cried and grieved because of the suffering. I was not eating much because I felt as if I was dead. I was left to wrestle with the never-ending question, *Why me?*

God Saved My Left Leg from Amputation

One day, while my legs were still in casts, I used a clothes hanger to scratch the back of my left hamstring and it ripped my skin off. Days later, my parents and siblings began to complain of smelling something foul and I didn't know what it was. (I even helped them to look for it.)

When my Mom looked at the back of my leg, she saw a huge infection! The lonely nights were horrific and the pain that I felt was like a knife drilling through my skull. The muscle spasms were as deep as hell and back. I wanted to take a knife and drill it through my heart repeatedly until I was dead.

My Mom drove me to the hospital and the doctors informed her that there was a possibility of amputating my left leg because of the infection. I felt horrible, but I told my Mom that the battle is not ours but the Lord's. They did another surgery to prevent cutting off my left leg. I took a huge dose of Morphine to numb the pain and continued to pray.

Again, God was with me through another surgery and He refused to let my left leg be cut off! God was not done with His wonders in my life and I kept giving Him the glory through testimonies. They redid my leg casts and I was able to go home within two weeks. I began to thank God for saving my life and for not giving up on me. He never gives up on His children; He loves us all.

Chapter 5: Moving Out of the Projects

Moving to another Elementary School

We eventually moved from Brown Lee Road townhomes to Pebble Creek in Jackson Georgia. I was happy to be in a new home and was looking forward to hopefully making new friends. Just when I was getting used to the new school and the new faces in my school, we were transferred from Jackson Elementary to another elementary school.

Everyone at the new school was very different from the former school. My teacher, Mrs. Clark, was very strict but nice. I can clearly remember rolling into the classroom on my first day and how everyone looked at me in my wheelchair and cast. I had to do my work on the clipboard and my teacher looked at me very hard.

There was also a 'Parapro' in the room, Mrs. Murphy, who made sure that I had everything I needed including her personal help. Mrs. Murphy was a huge help to me and saw to it that I was never behind in my classwork. She never pushed me too hard.

Effects of the Dark Period of My Parents' Divorce

My parents' divorce was a very dark year for my family and I. As a matter of fact, it was the hardest and darkest period of my early life.

I was very insecure at this time and I did not understand the reason for the events that were unfolding. Neither did my siblings.

It was very heart breaking and challenging to see my father leave. Everyone was affected by his absence, but my older brother John was hurt the most.

Becoming a single parent left my Mom to raise four kids on her own. I wished my father had not left his family, because we were going through enough suffering. The harder my Mom worked, the more I could see her stress levels increasing, but she loved her kids and wanted us to have a future.

The cast eventually came off my left leg and I was told not to worry about any more surgeries. I was happy to receive some good news after enduring so much suffering.

For a while, in the same year, I continued to get in trouble and was constantly in and out of physical altercations. I was running over students with my wheelchair because I was tired of being annoyed by them. It seemed as if trouble would always find me and I constantly argued with students and started fights.

The Principal would call me into the office to find out why I was angry all the time. I tried to tell her it was because the students kept talking about me and, as a result, I behaved badly or fussed. I told her that the bottom line was that I felt as if no one really cared about me and the world was against me.

I finally swallowed my pride and started working hard in school. The students stopped fighting with me as they saw my hard work. Everyone was happy to see me not fighting, but learning with them. The lessons were hard, but I kept up the work and refused to fail.

My Mom always took us to Ms. Emma, our neighborhood babysitter, to watch over us. We acted badly every time she would come to get us and we would run from her. My Mom would chase after us as we kept running around the house until she eventually caught and punished us for our bad actions. My Mom wanted us to be better kids, but we were struggling with living without a father.

To make the situation even harder, my twin sister Destinee was in the same grade as my younger sister, Jayana. Destinee, like myself, has been held back in kindergarten, which made her very unhappy.

After living in Pebble Creek for a couple of years, we left the neighborhood because my Mom wanted to move to a new one. During this time, one of my Mom's sisters, Auntie Carla, passed away. I was very saddened by all these events in my life.

I felt that my life was already complicated enough and filled with constant sadness, but now my Mom had to lose someone close to her? We went to the funeral and had one last look at Auntie Carla. After they buried her, they served a meal and my Mom looked at the grave one last time before heading home.

Life at another Elementary School

Again, I tell you that the struggle was real as we had to move from Jackson, Georgia back to Flovilla, Georgia. We moved into a beautiful three-bedroom house; everyone was happy with the new house. My Mom worked hard for all of us and we even had our own bedroom.

We were back at my old school and I was back in a familiar setting. The school Principal remembered me and was pleasantly surprise to see that I had changed a lot since our last meeting. The teachers were also surprised to see a difference in me. In the past, I was bad and they got used to it. In the present, I was happy to be different and stronger because I was picked on.

I started praying more and I kept the faith. I felt like no one could bring down my spirit and that school felt like a second home to me. I made some friends over those years and I will never forget them because they made me stronger when I was weak.

I still had the hatred and discrimination to deal with. As a result, I wanted to be dead and forgotten, but I had the support of my family. They kept pushing me to believe in miracles. The teachers were always hard on me, but I knew that I needed them because they refused to let me be a failure in this world.

Jesus within me made me feel like I was the light in darkness and the peace in the midst of chaos. I was learning a lot of things about the world and the schools were making me understand the world even more.

Moving Back to an Elementary School in Jackson

We eventually moved back to Jackson Elementary School, but I had finished my 4th grade year. My teacher was Mrs. Taylor and she was an African American female with a pointed nose and wore glasses. Mrs. Taylor was a great teacher; she loved teaching the young students and talking about their dreams.

I told her about my life struggles such as living without my father and I told her that I missed him so much. I told her that his coming by to check on us was not enough.

My other teacher was Mr. Douglas. Mr. Douglas was tall with brown eyes and short hair. He was one of my hardest teachers, but one of the most helpful. But I'll tell you more about him later.

Chapter 6: Taking Hold of Hope and Persevering

My Dream of Becoming a Wrestler

The students used to laugh at my dream of becoming a wrestler and called me all kinds of names. I hated them because they felt superior to me. They always used my physical condition to tell me about the impossibility of my dreams. They would say things such as, "You will never accomplish those dreams, but you can keep on dreaming."

Tears would roll down my eyes as they provoked me to anger. I kept trying to achieve my dreams and I knew that I would achieve it.

To make matters worse, Mr. Douglas was a hard teacher who hated to repeat things. I always had to ask him to repeat something and some of the students grew tired of my asking. As a result, Mr. Douglas began writing everything on the board.

The Advice of a Wise Teacher

One day, I asked Mr. Douglas about achieving the impossible and I told him that I wanted to achieve my dreams. I also told him that I did not have the strength to keep away the doubts. He talked to me about being strong in hard times. He said:

> *"You may be weak in front of your friends, but you have to get some courage. We all have to look deep inside ourselves and grab that hope and keep holding on to it."*

After I listened to the words of Mr. Douglas, I confronted the students. I told them that I was tired of them looking down on me and that I have dreams that none them could stop from coming true. I let them know that I might be different from them, but they needed to know that life was harder for me. (They actually listened to my speech.)

While everyone kept hating my dreams, I knew that Mr. Douglas's words of encouragement had given me the strength to go on; Mrs. Taylor's words had given me courage. These two teachers were good role models for me and I continue to pray for them.

The students did not change their ways, but I stayed away from their negativity. In this same year, I continued to pray and keep my faith in God. I also worked hard against all odds. My prayer for each day was:

> *"Heavenly father in heaven, I truly need Your strength and wisdom because the world is trying to bring me down. The bullying is getting out of hand and, as a result, I cry constantly about my condition and the pains of this world. The devil is trying to take my light and pull me into darkness.*
>
> *Father, You are the shield against that darkness. My whole world is against me, but I will always have You. You give me*

the strength to wake up and see another day. You put these challenges in my way to test my strength. The tests are very hard, but You are always with me. I need You to keep me on the right track because I do not want to fall off the track. You must keep me on this track and help me to cross the finish line. Amen."

I ended up in the TAG (Talented and Gifted) classes; I was working my way to the top. Everyone believed I should be in Special Education classes, but I proved them wrong with my placement test scores. Students were shocked to see me in these classes and talked about me. As they kept on talking, I refused to listen or talk to them. My family, who always knew I was smart, was proud of me.

The gifted classes were a lot harder than normal classes. The teachers were stricter and held us to a higher standard. For example, you were blessed to see less than ten assignments per class. We also had three projects a month and they had to be presented in front of the class.

In the beginning, I was a little nervous, but I tried my best and wished for the best. At the end, the students were clapping for me and they stopped talking about me. I made some good friends for life among them.

The teachers always asked about my writing because it was hard to read. They eventually understood my writing and stopped calling for me to explain what I wrote. Very often, I stayed for tutoring after school and I worked hard with Mrs. Taylor and Mr. Douglas.

Learning to Write Properly

At the same time that Mr. Douglas was working with me, Mrs. Taylor was helping with my handwriting. We started from the very basics of writing and reciting the Alphabets. I then started writing short stories with simple sentences and moved onto complex sentences.

My writing was becoming a little better, but it was still hard to read. I went back to writing short stories. I finally started writing decently and Mrs. Taylor was happy for me and wished me the best in my future. I will keep her words hidden in my heart till the end of my life.

During this particular year, I knew that against all odds, God was about to do something great for me. God made a way for me to attend regular courses and I was doing a phenomenal job. I was happy to be in normal classes and not be placed in special education classes. I thanked God for His help because we can do all things through Christ. Also, school was becoming easier for me and I realized that I just needed to keep believing in myself and staying out of trouble.

God's Help in My Class Presentation

I was working on my homework and forgot to work on my presentation. I immediately started working on the presentation because it was worth two test grades. As a result, I put my whole heart and soul into the project.

The sun was coming up and I was still putting the finishing touches on it with the hope that everyone would like the presentation. When they finally called my name and I walked to the board, I became very nervous to the point that my mind drew a blank.

After three minutes of staring at the walls, I began presenting my project and, at the end, everyone clapped for me. The teacher was happy that I worked so hard and wanted everyone to work as hard as I did.

Living on Food Stamps

Everything was going very well in our lives at home but, unbeknownst to me, something bad was about to happen. I knew that all goodness could not happen without something bad occurring in my family. To prove it, my Mom lost her job and her divorce became final.

Mom had been working hard for all of us, but she was fired from her job. We were worried about our living condition and the real possibility of being homeless. We started praying for a miracle because we really needed one.

After several months of trying to hold onto what we had, we were forced to live off food stamps. I never wanted to live off food stamps, but we had no choice. The food stamps guaranteed our survival, so we kept using them. The refrigerator and freezer were always full of food and I ate all kinds of foods. The family had hit rock bottom, but we were still praying to God for a breakthrough.

We always prayed in the good times, sad times, hard times and worst times, because we believed that being alive was a blessing. The times were getting very rough and things were only getting harder for us. My father was in and out of jail for various reasons, but I still loved him and missed the times with him. We had tons of fun and, most of the times that I was suffering from different aches and pains, my father was always with me.

My father would watch movies with me and keep me company. The times were not the best of times because I feared my father due to the constant beatings. My father was a good man at heart and I wished the divorce did not happen, but I could still talk to him. He would check on me from time to time.

The memories I have about him are always with me and I refuse to forget them. My best memories were watching football with my father and both of us cheering for the same team. The house would become very loud, but we were enjoying our lives.

Chapter 7: Moving Back to the Projects
The Pain of Being Evicted from Our Home

Things got worse for us and our situation became sadder than before. I was sleeping in my room and dreaming of good times to come, when my mother called everyone to her room. As we walked into the room, she immediately began crying because we were being evicted from our house! I had a lot of good memories here plus the fact of having my own room.

We had been very happy about owning our home and not living in a townhouse. I took pleasure in talking about living in my house. Once again I would have to leave a good neighborhood and friends to go back to Brown Lee Townhouses.

My Mom did not want to move back to a townhouse or the projects, but she had no choice. We were blessed to live in our house for a couple years and I thank God because we could have been living on the street. God does not put on us more than we can bear.

My mother called the movers to come and move all of our belongings. After the long days of moving, we were back at Brown Lee Townhouses. My Mom thanked God for all of His blessing and she never complained about the struggles.

Negative Reactions to My Desire to Play Football

The summer of that particular year was a special one for me, because I asked my Mom to let me play football. My Mom responded with a flat out NO! My Mom's reasoning was that she did not want me to get hurt. I thought about her response for a couple of days.

Everyone that I talked to about my desire to play football thought I was crazy. My Dad thought it was insane and my sisters thought it was impossible.

My First Personal Trainer Was My Big Brother

My big brother John knew I had what it took to play the game, because he saw within me the aggressive nature needed for the game. (Also, from our frequent fights, he had tested my strength.) As a result, he started training me because he believed in my desire to play football.

We started with weights. I would pick up the weights and try my best to hold onto them, but they kept falling to the ground. My brother John told me to be patient and not to rush the training. I tried a second time and, with some patience, I was finally able to lift the weights over my head!

I could see that my big brother was proud of me, so I kept trying harder because of his encouragement. We moved to the next level of training, because he wanted to build my arm muscles by engaging me in arm wrestling. Although I was very tired the first day, I agreed to the arm wrestling and my brother beat me five times in a row. I was getting too tired to continue so we stopped, but I truly wanted to beat my big brother because he believed in me.

I have always tried to do my best in everything that I do. The next morning, we had a rematch and we were both sweating from the struggle, but I kept pushing for the victory. My big brother lost and I finally won a match!

I felt better prepared in the last of the workouts and the final one was pushing off the wall or 'wall push-ups'. I moved to the wall and started the 'wall push-ups' as my big brother watched over me. When I was getting very tired and sweating from the stress, he encouraged me to finish the workout and I listened to him.

The window was blowing colder air compared to the night before and my big brother closed the window again and locked it. I was happy to have my big brother because he was always helping me.

My big brother gave me some cereal and milk in the morning and we were off to do 'wall push- ups'. My big brother was cheering me on and he made me tough; he pushed me to be stronger. I continued to do the 'wall push-ups' every day and did not complain.

My Big Brother the Athlete

My big brother played football and baseball and always shared his experiences with me. He told me about his love for the game, the nature of the sport and his accomplishments. My brother was the pitcher and he was known for throwing 50 mile balls.

The rival team could never hit a homerun. Sometimes they would smack the ball and it would fall to the ground. My brother would toss the ball to his teammates and tag them out. They had the best team because everyone was having fun. As a result, I always wanted to play sports, but I was not physically able to. My big brother's team won most of the games but, even though they lost at the finals, he had fun playing with all the teams and looked forward to another great year.

Football was a lot harder than baseball. My big brother played the punt return. He was the best player of the game and he liked his position on the field. During one of their games, they kicked the ball and it landed in my brother's hand and he began running for his life, but the opposing team caught him. The second time was a lot better, as my big brother caught the ball again. It turned out to be the best play of his life and it was a winning play.

It was awesome to watch my big brother running from left to right as the tacklers were pursuing him. They got tired as this continued and mistakenly left the middle field open. My big brother seized the opportunity and scored a touchdown with four tacklers chasing him! Everyone was cheering for him and shook his hand. I knew then that I had to play the game.

Playing Football and Winning the Game

I was reading the newspaper one day when I came across the story of a man named Kyle Maynard. He had no arms or legs, but he was a state champion in wrestling and played football! The newspaper article also talked about his other achievements in life. I read the article from beginning to end.

I realized that Kyle Maynard was just like me but he *made it*. I began thinking about my own possibilities. I told my Mom that if he could do it, I could too. My Mom thought about it and started reading news articles about Kyle Maynard. I eventually persuaded my mother to let me play and we drove to the recreation park to speak with the manger named Kenny Sims. My Mom asked him if her son could play and he quickly said no, but later said yes. I received the green light to play football and was excited that my brother and sisters could come to watch me play.

I was playing the guard. The guards basically tackle people and try to stop the ball. During one of our games, I tripped one of the runners that was coming from the right and I stole the ball. We scored our first point and the coach was proud of my determination. He let me play till the end of the game.

My Mom was there and she recorded the game for future memories. My brother and sisters were also there and they were happy for me. They kept cheering me on and I told them to keep believing in me. During the rest of the game, the other team was trying to steal the ball, but I tackled the player and retrieved the ball. The game moved into overtime because the scores were 14 to 14.

As the game went on, I could hear my Mom cheering louder and louder because she loves me with all her heart. She loves all her children with all her heart and she prayed for me because she finally saw me enjoying life.

My team was preparing the winning shot and I was the tackler. They were trying to stop the runner. I tackled them and stopped their advance. My team won the game and they cheered for me. My family hugged me and the coach told me to stay strong and never forget to believe in myself. After that game, I began to believe that nothing could take my happiness from me. However, just like usual, I spoke too soon.

Chapter 8: Life in the 5th Grade

Needing a Place to Call Home

Once again, we had to move from our house. We packed our bags and prepared for the next house in Jackson Square. By this time, I was in the 5th grade and I was tired of moving from place to place. We never stayed in one place long and I truly wanted a place to call home.

We had to attend another elementary school in Jackson. With so many people doubting my abilities, I had to fight for my rights and I had to fight my way onto the football field. I cannot count how many times I had people doubting my abilities that year. Everyone kept telling me the same thing and I got tired of hearing them. They discriminated against me because of my medical condition.

I had to keep the tears from flowing as they kept hurting my feelings. I took comfort in **2 Chronicles 32:8**:

> *"With him is an arm of flesh; but with us is the LORD our God to help us, and to fight our battles. And the people rested themselves upon the words of Hezekiah king of Judah."*

Overcoming the Mockers in the Classroom

My 5th grade teacher was named Mrs. Reese and she was my favorite teacher. She was very nice and always had a smile on her face. Mrs. Reese never laughed at any student's dreams because she believed that we all needed to dream for dreams were the only things that gave hope.

I agreed with her that we all needed hope in this world because some people will hurt your feelings with their words. I remembered her asking me, "What do you want to be when you grow up?" I said that I wanted to be an inspirational athlete and the class laughed at me. I felt worthless as a result, but I kept the faith even though I was crying on the inside. The students were saying to me, "You will never be an athlete; you need a reality check. We have a better chance than you because we can walk on two feet and you are stuck rolling."

The words were not only getting more hurtful, they were also getting more aggressive. For example, they would say, "The world doesn't need losers like you. Athletes are chosen from the best and not the worst. They are hard workers in their sports. They would never choose someone like you. You can keep dreaming because dreaming about being an athlete is not like being one."

They reminded me of my condition on a daily basis, but I hung on to the Word of the Lord in **2 Chronicles 32:7**:

> *"Be strong and courageous, be not afraid nor dismayed for the king of Assyria, nor for all the multitude that is with him: for there be more with us than with him."*

Mrs. Hamlin and Mrs. Baldridge were the 'Parapros' who pushed me to do my work and kept me on track.

Sometimes, when I got distracted in class and associated with the troublemakers, they would tell me to listen to them. I always tried my best to understand the classwork and I would ask for help when I needed it. The 'Parapros' would immediately come to explain the work to me.

Sometimes, I have to hear the Math problem again and see all the steps involved in the solution. I was not ashamed to ask for help because I would rather know the subject being taught than be an idiot. I knew that every classroom has a couple of idiots, but I refused to be one of them.

The students tried to stop me with their words and I worked that year to prove them wrong. I was school and sport wise so I decided to stay up a lot of nights to work on my subjects. For example, formulas would be all over the place and I would forget critical steps. I would read the textbook and reread the whole lesson for hours before moving to the next step. I was encouraged when I solved ten problems in the textbook without cheating by peeking at the answers in the back of the book.

My handwriting was the next one. On the same night, I took three pieces of paper and slowly wrote letters on them. When my writing looked legible, I went to sleep. I did this almost every night and I lost three hours of sleep each night.

My language art teacher, Mrs. H, always got on me about my writing. The very first grade she gave me was a 50! I was devastated with the grade so I became determined to not fail the class. Mrs. H told me to work on my writing because my words were hard to read. As a result, I forced myself to write fifty words a day and my words began to be more and more legible.

Mrs. H was happy with my writing and my grades went up. I worked extremely hard to get my grades up and she had tons of extra credit assignments. After days of doing extra credit and studying all night, my grades finally were at a satisfactory level.

Football Season Again in a New School

Football practice was a test of faith and determination. I told myself that having confidence was vital to being successful. I viewed having confidence as making a statement and gaining respect.

During my first day on the field, people started looking at me strange and said to me, "What are you doing here?" I said, "I am here to play football." They all laughed at me and told me to go home, but I said, "NO and I am here to stay. I'm not giving up on my dream of playing football."

The name of our team was Blue Hawks and our coaches were Kid Shepard, Henry Smith and Michael Carter. The very first day of practice was windy, but we refused to turn back. We all listened to the coaches about all of the plays and directions. The other players moved to their assigned positions. I moved to my position and waited for the play to begin.

When the first play started, we were fighting for the football. One person would be running with the ball and others would tackle him. I was trying to get my first tackle and I really wanted it but I failed. For the next play, the quarterback tossed the ball to the runners and they jumped over me. Another player tackled the player and scored a point. I failed a second time at a tackle.

We kept redoing the plays and I began to get tired, but I stayed in my position and kept trying. When the coaches saw my determination, they kept me on the field. I had to do something to prove to all of the players that I could play with the best of them. When the runner was coming from the right side, I tried to tackle him but I missed him by three seconds. I was so close to getting my first tackle.

In the next play, the players were moving back to the middle. I was in the middle and we had one last chance to win. The opposition was determined to score, but I was determined to stop the runner in order to earn respect from my team.

The quarterback threw the ball, the player caught the ball and saw an opening in the middle - **me**! I was waiting on the player and I smacked the ball. My team began cheering for me and, from that day on, started respecting me a little more. Coach Shepard called me to the sidelines and told me and Nyj Smith to line up in the back. In my head, I was afraid, but that *dog* in me was not. I told myself that I was unstoppable.

Another first play started and we moved to our positions. The quarterback tossed the ball and Nyj ran me over and the play continued. I knew I was going to make Nyj pay.

When the second play started, I had one target on my mind - Nyj. While everyone was moving to their spots, I hit Nyj. The players' faces were stunned from what they saw. From then on, Nyj began to respect me and stopped running me over.

Towards the end, the coaches came over to the players and announced that we had practiced enough for the day. As for me, I knew that our first game was coming up and I had to keep up my grades or I would not be allowed to play. I studied hard every night and kept praying to God. I trusted in His Word in **Hosea 14:9**:

> *"Who is Wise, and he shall understand these things? Prudent, and he shall know them? For the ways of the LORD are right and the just shall walk in them, but the transgressors shall fall there in."*

Finally, I finished my last homework assignment and was ready for my upcoming test. The first game would be after the test and my teacher would report my grades to the coaches, because the coaches could not let students with failing grades play. The next morning was my test. Everyone was having a hard time, but I was calm and not stressed. I passed with a test score of 88.

My teacher reported my grades to the coaches and they walked over and congratulated me. The big game was starting the next day and I could not wait to play. I was at home looking over the plays and studying as well. Again, I began to say to myself that everything was going my way and nothing could stop my happiness.

The day came and I headed out to the game. The players already had their uniforms on and I was putting on mine while everyone was shouting "Blue Hawks". The other team was cheering for the *Puppy Dogs*. Everyone was moving on the field and I watched them.

Both teams looked at each other and waited for the game to start. The first quarter began and the Blue Hawks scored the first point. The Puppy Dogs were preparing for their next play and I watched and cheered for my team.

The coaches changed the plays as they moved onto the second quarter. The Puppy Dogs had scored two touchdowns and the Blue Hawks were down by one touchdown; everyone was worried. The third quarter started and we scored a touchdown. Both teams had equal points and were tired.

As the fourth quarter began, I lost all hope of playing in the game, but I kept waiting for my turn. The Blue Hawks scored a touchdown and beat the Puppy Dogs. With only

40 seconds left in the fourth quarter, the coaches called my name and number and I moved onto the field. I went to the goal line and the other team's quarterback tossed the ball to a runner. The runner looked at the middle and saw an opening. I waited on the runner and tackled him.

My Mom screamed "ayeeeee" and everyone began shouting, "Berry made a tackle." The people in the crowd were stunned and started cheering for the Blue Hawks. The coaches were very happy as they cheered for me too. My brother John hugged me and said that he knew I had the strength to play football.

It proved that when the LORD gives you something, nobody can take it from you. My Mom took some pictures of the players and we headed to the house. I gained more respect from the other players including Nyj. I will never forget this memory for the rest of my life.

Me: A Local Hero

The next morning, I was joyful and the window was opened by the wind so I woke up to sunlight. I walked downstairs and was shocked when I saw the newspaper. I called all of my family members to come and see what I saw — **I made the local newspaper**! It said that *Devon Berry has the heart for football and the determination to be a great player.*

People were hugging my cousins and telling my family that I was the motivator of the team. I always say, "Don't stop getting it; get it as a cheer to get us pumped". I knew that although people said that it was impossible, God made it possible for me as stated in **Luke 1:37**:

"For with God nothing shall be impossible."

I played many more games and I had tons of fun. I ended up making the All-Stars' team. I made a name for myself because the All-Stars were the best of the best and I was one of the best. My teammates always cheered for one another and we never fought over little things. I loved playing on the All-Stars and I wished time would slow down, but I had to grow up. The fifth grade was over, but I always kept those memories.

Soon, I was officially a 6th grader. My goal was to make new friends and be the best that I could be.

Chapter 9: Life in the 6th Grade
Developing a Personal Motto: With God I Grind

On the first day of school, I met my new teacher, Mrs. Valentine. She was a Caucasian woman with blue eyes and was very nice. My 'Parapro' was Mrs. Hollingsworth.

At first, they doubted my abilities, but I proved them wrong when I did great on my test. It was challenging to become accepted by my new classmates, but I persevered as I stood alone. I humbled myself and did what I knew to do—grind (study hard). I call it WGIG (With God I Grind). I kept telling myself not to become worried because I was Devon Berry.

At this school, the students picked on me and made fun of me, but I refused to stop. I knew who I was and whose I was. Mrs. Valentine always gave pop quizzes and talked about being on time. She always said to us, "Never waste your time. You should live your dream to the fullest and do not let anyone hinder you. You have one life and you should not waste it". Students always listened to her words.

Mrs. Hollingsworth was a great 'Parapro'. During tough times, she always helped me, especially when the students were talking. Mrs. Hollingsworth would force them to stop and I was happy to have someone who could stop the bullies.

On one occasion, Mrs. Valentine gave a homework assignment to write a four-page essay. It was a sad moment for me because, as everyone was heading home, I began thinking about how hard the homework was going to be for me. I had always struggled to write and could not make friends easily. I only had a couple of real friends who watched out for me but, with this assignment, I was alone.

I did complete my paper. After playing some Madden with my brother John, I stayed up and worried about the essay I wrote, while everyone was sleep.

The Insensitive and Cruel Bullies

The next day, in Mrs. Valentine's class, we all had to present our essays to the class. I was the first to be called and, as I started talking about myself in my essay, I could see that the students were getting an understanding of my daily struggles and pains. At the end, they gave me a group hug. The other students also talked about their struggles but, when I left the classroom to go to lunch, some began calling me 'non- walker'. They kept on saying it, but I ignored them as I walked in the lunchroom and picked up my lunch.

My friends were waiting for me at the table and my sisters were watching as the students were calling me 'non-walker'. They rose up, confronted the bullies, defended their brother and stopped the name calling. I am happy to have two sisters that care for me and I look up to my big brother John who wanted me to be strong by pushing me to do my best.

I ate lunch with my friends and we talked about the upcoming quiz. My friends were preparing for the quiz that would be based on reading a book on Shakespeare so everyone pulled out their book and started reading. As the school day came to a close, I got on the bus and headed home.

At bedtime, the moon was still shining in the sky as I went to sleep, but the bullies were even in my dreams! In the dreams they kept saying 'non-walker' and they pushed me into a locker. When I woke up, I prayed to God to take away the nightmare and help me become stronger. In class that morning, we all turned in our homework and I knew that I was becoming a little stronger in spite of some of the students trying to keep me down.

Mrs. Hollingsworth looked at my homework and she noticed that my answers were correct. She was very proud of me, but I said to her, "I could not have done it without your help. You kept pushing me to do my best so I studied very hard."

Mrs. Valentine was also proud of the students and we were reading a new story in class. We were all given a book to read from and I was asked to read the first three chapters. Everyone was staring at me with scary eyes but I started reading the story and, after a while, the teacher told me to stop. She chose another student to read three chapters also. We read from the book for the entire class period. We were enjoying the story, but the bell rung so I decided to head back home to finish reading the story.

Bullies in My Dream

At night, Mom and everyone in the house came home late. We all went to bed and I could not wait to see my friends at school again, but I had another nightmare.

In this dream, the students laughed at me and called me 'non-walker'. This time, some of the teachers were saying 'non-walker' also. I was on the floor crying as the voices yelling 'non-walker', kept coming at me.

I woke from the dream with tears in my eyes but I was determined not to let them get to me. In reality, the next morning was a sad day for me because, as I was walking through the doors, the students started saying 'non-walker'. As I headed to my class, they followed me and kept saying, 'non-walker'. Mrs. Valentine stood up for me and got the students to leave the classroom.

A Lesson for Bullies

In class, we were working on a group assignment and my friends chose the story about bullies. I read some of the pages about a kid that was being bullied by his upperclassmen. His friends ran from him and the bullies beat him up. In the end, the kid had to stand up for himself and he told the truth when the Principal found out about the bullies. The bullies were taken from the school and jailed.

We all enjoyed the story. My friends made notes on the book and I made notes too, but the bell rang and we headed home.

When my friends shook my hands, I knew that the school year was going by quicker than the previous. We had only four more months to go and, because I enjoyed the year, my belief was that the next year could only get better. I looked at all my classwork for the year and I noticed that I had done a lot of hard work and praying. Prayers kept me from doing idiotic things throughout the year.

The next couple of months passed by fast and the school year came to an end. My sisters were ready for the New Year and I was happy to get to the end of the year. A New Year for me meant the start of spring training.

Chapter 10: Overcoming a Difficult Coach and Playing Football in the 6th Grade

The Coach Only Sees My Disability

When spring training came, I found out that our Coach was named David Akin and he was a big, muscular cop. He was also the Head Coach of the Middle School.

On the first day, he said to me, "What are you doing here?" I said, "I am playing football." He said, "You have a disability." I said, "I have the ability that God gave me. I will play football because in order to be something, you have to do something."

I thought to myself, *spring training is about to start and the coach is discriminating against me because of my condition.* Nevertheless, I kept believing in myself. We walked to the weight rooms and I started with the small weights with a plan to move to the heavier ones.

Instead of encouraging me, the coach kept telling me to quit, but I refused each time. I loved the sport with all my heart and soul and refused to let a coach stop me from enjoying it.

Weight Training with Heavier Weights

They placed the 20 pound weights in my arms and I picked them up with all my might as everyone watched. They noticed my progress, but the weights were a little heavier than before. I remembered some of my brother's words about surpassing your weakness.

"You have to keep training and remove the weakness. The world will keep trying to break you, but you must prove them wrong. I believe in you brother; keep doing your best."

I picked up the weights and felt stronger; the next weights were the thirties. They placed the weights in my hands as the coach watched. We kept training for two hours.

Even after the coach had closed the weight room and my Mom was driving me home, I kept thinking about surpassing my weakness and getting stronger. My sisters were waiting for me because they always worried about me, but they always kept me in their prayers.

When the lights were turned off and I went to sleep, I began to dream about playing football. In the dream, the players were doing some good plays and I was the guard. A runner jumped over a player and I tackled him and got the ball. My team ran the ball to a field goal and we scored the point. Everyone was happy and I woke up. I immediately headed to training.

The Key to Being a Successful Nose Tackle

The coach started the very first lesson of the practice. During the lesson he said to us, "You must learn to hold the line from runners." He taught us some other rules of the game.

Afterwards, everyone moved to their spots to stop the runners. I grabbed the shoe of the runner and fell on the ground. We started the training again and I needed to get some tackles for the night.

During the next play, the runner was coming from the right and I moved to the incoming player. I tackled the runner with a leg grab and the coach announced that the training was done for the day. We all went to the locker room and rested. We talked about the training for the next couple of days. As for me, I was drinking my energy drinks and eating some protein bars.

When I got home, I watched some football on TV. The teams were nearing the third quarter and I needed to see their moves on holding the line. The players were running through the middle and they tossed one of them. The game ended in a tie and they went into overtime, but I went to sleep thinking about the future. My desire was to be someone in the future; I needed to be remembered for something. I would hate to die and not be known for anything.

The very next morning was going to be the start of harder training. I ate some breakfast and prayed before my Mom drove me to school. In the field, the players were ready for the next part of the training and the coach gave everyone a handout saying, "You are going to move to that spot and wait on my commands." The students moved to their spots and the hard part for me was about to begin: I was assigned to tackle targets. The problem was that the targets would hit me right smack in the face.

My head hurt from being hit by targets. I learned to move out of the way and tackle from the back the next time the target came. When everyone was done learning their task, we moved to a practice game and we went to our positions. The quarterback threw the ball with all his might, but the ball was too high in the air. The wide receiver caught the ball and ran a touchdown; my team was down by seven points. I needed to play my role and stop the advancing of the ball.

The quarterback tried the same move and tossed the ball to the runner. I stopped the advance. My team cheered for my move as we moved the ball to the other side. Our quarterback tossed the ball to the runner and the runner was stopped by two big dudes. They tackled him on the ground and the runner was injured from the tackle. He sat on the sidelines and the coach called his parents.

I learned an important lesson in tackling: You must tackle with your teammates for easier tackles. The quarterback tossed another ball and the runner passed the ball from right to left. I double teamed the player with my teammate and the runner was down for the count — the game was over with a tie!

Everyone rested on the sidelines thinking about the plays. We needed to do better. Our plays were good, but we had to execute them better or we would lose the game.

At the next play, everyone paid more attention to the instructions for their roles and executed their play better. I was getting more tackles than before, but the wind was picking up and we were down for the day. The drive home was long and there was traffic on the road. I just wanted to sleep in my bed.

The next day of working out on the field, the coach saw some progress in the players. He kept pushing us and he stopped talking about me. When we went to the weight room, they placed 30 pound weights in my hands because I needed to master the weight or I would never grow stronger.

I picked up the weights and realized the increase in my muscle strength. My teammates also saw my strength increase and started working with me and not against me. I knew that I was being blessed.

Final Practice and Lessons Learned

At our final practice, everyone was holding hands and I prayed for my team and the coach. They had made me stronger and wiser and I asked God to protect and keep them. Everyone was back picking up weights and the coach had some encouraging words for the team. He said:

> *"We are having our last meeting tomorrow and you are my best group. I have been coaching for a long time and you have made a bond with each other. I want you all to be safe and prepare for the final meeting."*

When my Mom picked me up and asked about my experience, I told her about the bonding with the players and how we were enemies on the first day because of my disability. I told about the threats the students made, beating each other up and how we are now working together. I also told her that the coach was treating everyone better, how the hatred had left the building and we were loving the atmosphere. My Mom was so proud of me and wished me the best.

I was ready for the last training. My teammates were shaking hands and waiting for the coach to come in. When the coach came, he gave us another speech:

> *"I wish all of you the best in your future. You are all destined for greatness. Don't let this world put you down."*

We walked to the field and kept the words in our hearts. I was back to guarding the line in the front as the quarterback threw the ball to the left. The runner was coming fast from the left, I caught his shoe lace and tackled him. He jumped off the ground and told me to *keep that up.*

I kept tackling the runners and getting the ball. We finally got the ball and the runner jumped over the players, scored the first point and we kept on scoring. Everyone was getting tired at the end of the game and we walked to the locker room for water. The coach shook our hands before we left the school.

My Mom picked me up with a smile. I missed being on the field and I missed the players. I hoped that we would all see one another again the next year in the 7th grade.

Chapter 11: Life in the 7th Grade

Going to the Movies

I knew that my family would always have my back. We all had good grades because of our mother. She was always pushing us to be smart. I will never speak against my mother because she has my back like no one else. My Mom would drive us to the movies and we watched two movies as a family. I loved all of our family moments. We had a fun times at the movies; that I will always cherish.

We knew that we had to cherish these memories because death could come at any time. Unfortunately, we had to move back to the projects at Brown Lee Road so we went there to clean the house. This move also meant changing schools.

The Good Dream

I was preparing for the 7th grade and, the day before school started, me and my siblings looked at one another with smiles. We have made it another year in school with only five more years to go.

Although I had some trouble with the coach and certain students, I overcame them all. As a result, I can say that my 6th grade year was great. I was ready for all of the future challenges and struggles. While in this mindset, I had the best dream ever.

In the dream, everyone was looking up to me and they understood my life struggles. They wanted to see me grow as a person and I was taking pictures with a lot of people, including students. I woke up knowing that I was blessed to have made it that far. I vowed to never forget my faith and resolved to keep praying to my God. He had never turned His back on me.

First Day at Another School

On the first day of 7th grade, students at the new school were running to the tryouts. The coaches challenged me and put me through all kinds of tests, more than other players. I thought they hated seeing me and the players were just as bad. They would dump me in trash cans, but I did not lose faith. Also, school work was very challenging that year.

I kept giving my best to the team, but the coaches were always yelling at me. I always had to give more than one hundred percent. The players were not afraid to bully me. I could cry from all the bullying, but I knew that I would get through it.

As the players continued to bully me, I rose up one day and stood my ground. I told them that I was tired of being thrown in trash cans and I let them know that they could bully me all they wanted to, but I would not give up on my dreams. The bullies began to back off, but I was embarrassed of not being my best at practice. Somedays, I felt like only ten percent of myself.

Being an Idiot

My classes were very hard that year and they required a lot of studying. Also, I was written up for sexual harassment for touching girls' butts. To make matters worse, I was back to fighting a lot.

In spite of all these things, I kept my grades up. My teachers were amazed at how smart I was and I continued to prove them wrong about me. I could remember a time when I cursed out my teacher and she wrote me up. The coaches were about to kick me off the team, but they gave me another chance. I was blessed by not being kicked off the team because I prayed to my God to let them give me another chance. I told God that I was being an idiot by cursing out my teacher. I acknowledged that I was in the wrong and that she was trying to help me. I asked God for forgiveness.

As I was heading home, I began to write an apology letter to my teacher for my bad behavior saying,

> *"You just wanted me to be my best and I cursed you out. I hope you accept this apology. You are one of my best teachers and I hope you teach for many years."*

I signed the letter and, on the next day, I walked up and handed her the apology letter. The teacher was happy to receive the letter and she called me to her desk saying, "You are one of my best students."

I stopped being rude in class and listened to the words of my teacher. We were learning about science and the body parts. I took a lot of notes and I prepared to study later. Later that day, the coaches called for the players. I walked to the locker room armed with **Hebrews 11:1**:

"Now faith is the substance of things hoped for, the evidence of things not seen."

The coaches called everyone and moved us to the field. We practiced some plays and I waited for the play. The quarterback tossed the ball into the crowd and I moved to the spot and tackled the players. The coaches thought that I was lucky with the tackle because they did not respect my work.

We did the play for a second time and I missed the tackle. After this, they told me to practice my tackle on targets and they placed the targets in front of me. While the others were practicing their plays on the field, I was tackling targets.

At the end of the day, my Mom picked me up and I went home to study for my quiz the next day. The quiz was on the parts of the brain and I scored an 85. I prayed to God saying, "I need your strength to get better in football. I truly want to do my best and show the world Your miracle. Amen."

Balancing Class Work with Football Practice

The next lesson was on the organs of the body. We watched a movie on the body and its parts and were given handouts. We had to write down all of the organs in the body and their functions. At the same time, I had to go to the field for football practice. It meant that I had to work very hard and I passed the assignment.

The next lessons were on the brain and the cells in the body. We watched a PowerPoint presentation and I took notes. My teacher passed out an essay paper; we had to write four pages on the PowerPoint presentation. After the class was over, the only thing on my mind was the upcoming football game, but I also had to focus on my studies.

The game was about to start and all the player walked to the locker room to put on their uniforms. The coaches gave the players instructions on the plays, but I was sitting on the sidelines. I had to watch most of the game from the sidelines.

The coaches finally called me and told me that I needed to tackle the players and stop them from scoring. I knew I was ready to play my part. Therefore, when the quarterback passed the ball and the runner was coming my way, I tackled him with all my strength. We won and the coaches were happy with the play. They congratulated the players and we had some pizza in the gym.

When I went to sleep that night, I dreamt of being a failure. In the dream, the whole world was against me and people were telling me to stop trying. They were saying, "You are destined to be nothing in this world. The world is better without losers." The people kept on shouting these words and their voices were getting louder. The dream finally ended and I woke up.

When I got to school, my teacher was happy with all of the great work I was doing and we all were ready to move to the next lesson on the bones in the body. We watched a movie on the types of bones and took notes in preparation for the quiz that would follow.

My teacher handed everyone the quiz and I took my time working on it because I wanted to do my best. I watched as some of the other students were rushing through the answers. While we were waiting for our grades, I was wondering about the next game. The whole class passed the quiz.

The next big game was going to be in two weeks so we were back in the weight room. They placed the 35 pound weights in my hands and I pushed them up. Sweat started to run down my hands because they were heavier, but I endured all of the pain and made it to the end of training.

The day of the game finally arrived and we moved to our positions on the field. When the quarterback tossed the ball to a teammate, they tricked the players and runner went the other way. The runner was right beside the line but he never crossed over. We learned a new move from this game. I headed to my house to prepare for my test the next morning. I needed to pass this test so that I could prove to everyone that stood against me that they were wrong about me.

The students were very scared when the teacher passed out the test, which consisted of 50 questions. The teacher gave everyone until the end of the class to finish it.

Again, I took my time to read all of the questions and I answered them according to my best knowledge. The hard questions were in back of the test while the easy ones were in the front. I answered all of the easy ones and I took a three-minute break before starting on the hard questions.

Everyone turned in their paper with stress on their faces and we waited in complete silence. When the teacher handed back all of the tests, I scored 89! I kept my score to myself as I left the class.

Chapter 12: The Discovering New Sports

Joining the Wrestling Team

The next day, we had no football practice so I relaxed for the day. As I was walking to one of my classes, I noticed the wrestling team. It looked very hard, but I wanted to try out for the team.

I walked to the wrestling room and I tried out. I was accepted, but many of them were surprised to see someone like me. My first match was very hard, because I was trying to hold down my opponent, but he kept moving from left to right. The opponent eventually got away from me and he came back to have me in a chokehold.

I was forced to surrender the match so I went to drink some water and watch the others wrestle. I found out that the other wrestlers were all using the chokehold and they were not afraid to tell you about it. I watched as two wrestlers were moving back and forth in the ring for 10 long minutes. They both refused to be the loser, but someone eventually had to tap out.

I Sucked at Wrestling

I went into my second round for the day. My opponent was very scary and he kept cracking his knuckles. I moved to hold him down, but something was messing me up. My opponent stopped my advance by holding me in his chokehold.

I could not stay in the ring so I immediately gave up the match. I noticed that everyone was cheering for me, but I needed one more round to help me learn the basics of the game. The others were brought into the ring and I recorded some of the wrestling because I needed the data to help me become a better wrestler.

The longest time in the ring is 20 minutes. I was back in the ring for a third time and my opponent was bigger than the others, but I tricked him with a fake chokehold. He then came to my side and I held his arms in an attempt to make him surrender. He was stronger than me and pushed me off. I fell to the ground and hurt my hands. My opponent had me in an arm hold and I gave up the round.

I watched the final round as the wrestlers came back in the ring to finish the match. In the ring, the student on the right was trying to hold the leg of the student on the left. The student on the left was caught off guard and the student on right student held him in a neck hold. The student was forced to give up the match. The wrestling was done for the day and it was not my best day. I held on to **Psalms 71:14**:

> *"But I will hope continually, and will yet praise thee more and more."*

I sucked very badly at wrestling and I lost every one of my matches, but I always gave it my all. Although people talked about me, I never gave up my ambition. I finally headed home with some pains and I laid in my bed. My homework had to be done by the morning, but the pain was too much.

I prayed before falling asleep; I prayed for all the good things that were happening to me and against the bad things. I woke up to do my homework because it was 10 pages. At school that day, I turned in my homework and we began to learn about the different types of muscles in the human body. We were handed a packet on the muscles of the body with instructions that we were going to learn the materials in it over the next five weeks.

Joining the Wheelchair Racing Team

The homework was to read the materials in the first week. I knew that I could not slack on the homework, but I wanted to test something. I was going outside when I noticed the wheelchair race. I tried out for the Track Team and I did track wheelchair racing.

In my first wheelchair race, I was the underdog but I never stopped grinding (pushing myself hard). They placed us on the track and I waited for them to start the race. Everyone was moving superfast and I was the rocket. I began to move with all my strength in great speed as I tried to catch up with them, but they knew the track better than me. We finished the first lap and still had three more laps to go, but I was slowly moving up the ranks.

The racers were watching as my speed increased and caught up with them. I passed a racer and we were sweating in our wheelchairs, but we were having fun. We finished the second lap and the third lap was the lap of serious movements. The racers were breaking each other and I was at the back. My hands were getting a little tired, but I moved up the ranks and made it to fourth place.

I was still the rookie in the group, but they respected my competitive abilities. As for me, I had fun and made some memories. I headed back to the house to study my classwork and I stayed up to read the whole packet. I also made some notes on the pages before going to sleep. I wanted to race the players again because I had so much fun and no one was against me on the team.

I woke up very early and went to school. My teacher handed us the quiz on the first part of the packet and I was very tired from racing the previous day, but I refused to sleep in class. Instead, I asked the teacher for a bathroom break.

I went to the bathroom, cleaned my eyes and I kept myself awake. I went back into the class room and finished taking the quiz. After class, I wanted to stay for the wheelchair racing, but I was too tired so I went home. I started studying for my upcoming quiz on the second part of the materials in the packet and it was a lot harder than the first. I had to reread all the materials and I made detailed notes. I was happy to be done and I went to bed. The second wheelchair racing was starting the next day and I needed to be there.

Placing 2nd in Wheelchair Racing

After I took the quiz in class, I headed to the wheelchair racing. We lined up for the race and I wanted to be the winner or in second place. In the first lap, I passed three of the racers and kept racing with all my strength. The tables had turned: they had to catch up to me, but I kept moving faster.

The leader was three racers in front of me and we were on the second lap. My hands seemed to be reaching their limits, but I believed God would make a way for me and not fail me. He answered me and suddenly, my hands were not as tired and I kept racing to victory.

During the third lap, I was finally in the second place and the leader was keeping his distance from me, but I stayed on him. We began racing neck and neck for the final lap and he pushed himself an inch forward to get to first place. I was in second place, but I had a great race.

Everyone was tired from the race: my hands and arms were very sore, but I loved having fun and breathing the fresh air during the race. The wheelchair racing also took away some of the negative thoughts in my head.

When Mom asked me about the race, I told her about the fun I had and how I challenged the racers. I was back in my room and I looked over the class materials in the packet. I remembered most of the material and figured that I was fine for the next day's quiz. While sleeping, I had a dream of being chased by the football players. In my dream, the football players were beating me, throwing me in trash cans and I was defenseless and bleeding.

The next day in class, when my teacher handed out the quiz, I was not worried because I knew that the test could not get any harder. I looked at the questions and started writing my answers. I guessed the answers to the last five questions because they were too hard. At the end, I had a good feeling about the scores.

Everything was looking good and we were headed towards the summertime, but my life at home was still very rough. My Mom was working her one job and getting child support. Although she was also getting my disability check, she was barely making ends meet. We had no air condition and, sometimes, we did not know where we were going to lay our heads. But Mom kept us in church.

We are a church family and we prayed every Sunday for a blessing to come. We never gave up on our God because He has All-power. We trusted in His Word in **Psalm 71:1-20:**

"In thee, O LORD, do I put my trust: let me never be put to confusion. 2 Deliver me in thy righteousness, and cause me to escape: incline thine ear unto me, and save me. 3 Be thou my strong habitation, whereunto I may continually resort: thou hast given commandment to save me; for thou art my rock and my fortress. 4 Deliver me, O my God, out of the hand of the wicked, out of the hand of the unrighteous and cruel man. 5 For thou art my hope, O Lord GOD: thou art my trust from my youth. 6 By thee have I been holden up from the womb: thou art he that took me out of my mother's bowels: my praise shall be continually of thee. 7 I am as a wonder unto many; but thou art my strong refuge. 8 Let my mouth be filled with thy praise and with thy honour all the day. 9 Cast me not off in the time of old age; forsake me not when my strength faileth. 10 For mine enemies speak against me; and they that lay wait for my soul take counsel together, 11 Saying, God hath forsaken him: persecute and take him; for there is none

to deliver him. 12 O God, be not far from me: O my God, make haste for my help. 13 Let them be confounded and consumed that are adversaries to my soul; let them be covered with reproach and dishonour that seek my hurt. 14 But I will hope continually, and will yet praise thee more and more. 15 My mouth shall shew forth thy righteousness and thy salvation all the day; for I know not the numbers thereof. 16 I will go in the strength of the Lord GOD: I will make mention of thy righteousness, even of thine only. 17 O God, thou hast taught me from my youth: and hitherto have I declared thy wondrous works. 18 Now also when I am old and grayheaded, O God, forsake me not; until I have shewed thy strength unto this generation, and thy power to everyone that is to come. 19 Thy righteousness also, O God, is very high, who hast done great things: O God, who is like unto thee! 20 Thou, which hast shewed me great and sore troubles, shalt quicken me again, and shalt bring me up again from the depths of the earth."

After Sunday service, we went back home with the words of the preacher still fresh in our minds. I kept praying to God for my breakthrough. I knew that God was slowly giving it to me. I could not wait for my 8th grade year because I knew that it was a blessing for me to make it that far in a world that was growing more evil.

My big brother told me to do my best in high school because he wanted me to have a bright future. I took – and still do - all of his advice and use it in my daily life. Most importantly, I want to make my mother proud by not being a failure. I believe that she has done too much for our family to watch it fall by the wayside.

Chapter 13: Life in the 8th Grade

The Year I Did Not Play Football

The New Year finally came and, just like that, I was an 8th grader! I was so proud and I believed that it was going to be my best year yet. I was ready to play football again, but the coach told me not to play and my Mom agreed with him. As a result, my 8th grade year was the only year that I barely played football. I concentrated on my studies because education is more important to me than any sport.

Learning Difficult Math Problems

I had a very strict math teacher who always came into the classroom with a bad attitude, but we still respected her. On the first day of class, she walked around and asked us our names. She made everyone stand up and say something about themselves. She brought out the textbooks and gave one to each student, but when the students began talking while she was teaching, she handed out a pop quiz.

Everyone pulled out their paper and prepared to take the quiz as she wrote the questions on the board. We had a total of eight minutes to solve the problems. I answered the first eight out of ten questions. The last two questions were too hard so I refused to waste my time on them. My teacher walked around the room and picked up the pop quiz papers. After this, we *never* talked again while she was teaching.

Her pop quizzes were very hard and I passed the first one with a score of 75. I knew then that it was not good for me to be starting out with a low grade, so I decided to work harder. The first lesson began with formulas. She explained that we needed the formulas because they were the basis for the work that we would do in class.

The practice math problems in my homework were very long and I had to show all of the steps as I solved them. We could not just show the answers, but we had to show the steps it took to get to the answers. (I showed my work and the steps to the solutions on four pages.)

While doing my homework, the hateful words from the students at school flooded my mind and it took all of my mental strength to complete the homework. The next day, I turned in my assignment, but the teacher had another pop quiz waiting for us.

Everyone pulled out their paper and pencils in preparation for the quiz. The questions were just like the homework and I was determined to score 100. I began with the first question and I had to show all the steps in my answers. At the end, everyone was waiting on me to finally finish and turn in my paper.

My teacher started teaching more complex math problems and she wrote all the steps on the board. As the math questions were getting more difficult, the steps were also getting longer; they actually doubled. Everyone was exhausted from her lessons.

New Bullies in the 8th Grade

After class, I was getting some water from the fountain, when some students bombarded me, calling me bad names and cursed at me. I eventually left the water fountain and went to my locker. Also, when I said a few words about myself in class and shared my dream, they laughed at me.

When it was time for the first football game, the football team began saying to me, "Look at the one with all the disabilities who wanted to play with us, but the coach denied him." I held back the tears; I hated being told what I could not do.

As the football players were running to the locker room, I told them, "I will be playing next year and that is a promise. You will see me next year and I will be playing." The football players laughed at me and proceeded to the locker room. My Mom was waiting for me and she drove me home.

Asking for Divine Help before Doing Homework

Before I started my homework that evening, I would read a little from my Bible. I focused on the message of John the Baptist in **Mark 1:2-15**:

"As it is written in the prophets, Behold, I send my messenger before thy face, which shall prepare thy way before thee.
3 The voice of one crying in the wilderness, Prepare ye the way of the Lord, make his paths straight.
4 John did baptize in the wilderness, and preach the baptism of repentance for the remission of sins.
5 And there went out unto him all the land of Judaea, and they of Jerusalem, and were all baptized of him in the river of Jordan, confessing their sins.
6 And John was clothed with camel's hair, and with a girdle of a skin about his loins; and he did eat locusts and wild honey;
7 And preached, saying, There cometh one mightier than I after me, the latchet of whose shoes I am not worthy to stoop down and unloose.
8 I indeed have baptized you with water: but he shall baptize you with the Holy Ghost.
9 And it came to pass in those days, that Jesus came from Nazareth of Galilee, and was baptized of John in Jordan.
10 And straightway coming up out of the water, he saw the heavens opened, and the Spirit like a dove descending upon him:
11 And there came a voice from heaven, saying, Thou art my beloved Son, in whom I am well pleased.
12 And immediately the Spirit driveth him into the wilderness.
13 And he was there in the wilderness forty days, tempted of Satan; and was with the wild beasts; and the angels ministered unto him.
14 Now after that John was put in prison, Jesus came into Galilee, preaching the gospel of the kingdom of God,
15 And saying, The time is fulfilled, and the kingdom of God is at hand: repent ye, and believe the gospel."

Prayers Works

In the 8th grade, I loved reading scriptures before studying, because it made my studying easier. It also helped to clear my mind of all the hateful words and forms of rejection.

Afterwards, I worked on the long math problems and I did not feel frustrated when I had to redo some of the steps, because I kept messing up. On one occasion, when I turned in the long tedious homework, I discovered that half of the class did not turn in theirs! The punishment? Another pop quiz and it was harder than the homework. When I looked at the first three questions, I noticed that they were super hard and the other students were looking at one another as they were trying to figure out the problem.

As for me, I immediately began to remember the hard problems from the homework; those were just like the ones before me. I knew that I could solve them because prayer works! After about 10 minutes of filling in the answers, everyone turned in their paper. We had to prepare for the next lesson and another upcoming test.

The next morning, when the alarm clock went off, I decided to do something different. I was going to read a whole chapter of the Bible and I chose 1 John Chapter 5, but I meditated on **1 John 5:14-15, 21**:

> *"**14** And this is the confidence that we have in him, that, if we ask any thing according to his will, he heareth us: **15** And if we know that he hear us, whatsoever we ask, we know that we have the petitions that we desired of him ... **21** Little children, keep yourselves from idols. Amen."*

In class, we waited anxiously as the teacher handed everyone a test packet. I was a little nervous because I knew that I was not the best test taker. The whole room was completely quiet during the test.

While some of the students were writing down formulas, I worked on the first section, which was from the first lesson. I then moved to the next section which was based on the second lesson but, at some point, I had to pull out the calculator because the numbers were too large.

The last part was the hardest one. I did half the work on the paper and the other half on the calculator. After several minutes of reviewing our answers, everyone turned in their test paper. When the bell rung, I could not wait to get to the football game. Our home team was winning in the first quarter, but the opposing team tied the game by the end of the second quarter. In the end, our home team won and the players were happy with the win.

Through it all, I would say that my 8th grade year was fun and enjoyable. The tests were very hard but I studied hard and the teachers were happy to see me in the school. I was glad to be moving up in the world because the 9th grade was only a couple of months away.

During the summer when we were out of school, we had family fun nights. Sometimes we played board games or Madden on the PlayStation for hours. I finally beat my brother at Madden and I kept beating him since. My best memory of my 8th grade year was watching the football games and all of my teachers who never talked down to me. They will always be in my heart and soul.

Chapter 14: Life in the 9th Grade

I Promised to Pass All My Classes

My sisters and I were very happy to be moving to the 9th grade. My brother helped convince my Mom to let me play football. As a result, my 9th grade year began with a great start.

I am so happy to have a brother that believes in me and never talks against me. I made my Mom a promise to pass all of my classes and to have the best year ever. My teachers were giving me tons of homework and projects and I stayed up late at night and studied for many hours. The projects were fun because I had to work with other people and we had to work together or we would fail.

I did most of the writing on the projects from reading books at the library while the others would go to the board and write the speeches. In other words, when my teacher was handing out projects, I usually choose one for our group and would go to the library and do the research. The others bought the boards and made the cards. They did the class presentation.

Partying with Friends

We had some good speeches in our class presentations and many of my classmates became my friends. Things were going on well for me because I was passing all my classes and my teachers were happy to see me. They called me a hard worker who cannot be hindered by discrimination. I began going to lot of parties and meeting a lot people. My friends were taking me to these parties where we had tons of fun.

I loved all of the partying, but I could not stay out too late because I always had homework and tests in morning. My studies always came first. My friends would party almost every weekend and their grades were going down. I had to stop partying with them because they were a bad influence.

Playing Football Again and Being on TV

I was officially on the football team and was part of the first training of the year. My teammates were not the best of people because they always tried to turn the coach against me. When I tried to explain myself, the coach would not listen. I wished that my teammates treated me better, but they only picked on me.

Once again, I had to endure bullying because I loved football with all my heart. I made up my mind that they could talk about me all day, but their words would not hurt me.

Life at home was very tough, but God spoke to me about great things to come. I kept listening to God and trusting in His ways because He alone makes possibilities out of disasters.

I can still remember when I got my first chance to be on TV and how my teammates doubted my abilities. As for me, I said that I can do all things through Christ. I knew that as long as I believed in the name of the LORD, I could do anything in the world.

We were playing against another team and the coach was still holding me back. He would not me let me play so I watched most of the game and waited for my moment. The coach called me in the fourth quarter, but I was very happy to be seen on TV.

When I moved to the field, everyone was surprised to see me. The other team was running their play and my goal was to hold the line and tackle the runner. The quarterback threw his best play and the runner came right in front of me. I immediately tackled him and everyone began cheering at my play, but my teammates were still looking at me with evil eyes. They hated being seen on the small field with me. I kept smiling in their faces as I played the rest of the game.

After the game, new sets of people began doubting me and telling me that I should not count on being anything in life just because I was on TV! They were showing their hatred towards me, but I never did anything to deserve their wicked treatment. After the game, I was back to reading the books and doing all of the research for my team. My friends were still buying the boards, making the cards and finishing the rest of the project.

Finally, we put the project together and presented it in front of the class. Everyone liked it.

Philippians 4:13 came to pass in my life:

"I can do all things through Christ who strengthens me."

Another Desire to Commit Suicide

As the year went by, many people still had no faith in me so I contemplated committing suicide. Only God stopped me from doing something crazy. I could have ended my life and put a huge burden on my family, leaving them to blame themselves for my death.

My brother would have felt that he failed me, whereas he had been in my corner since the beginning. I realized that I could not let the years of my brother's hard work and determination be for nothing. My Mom would have blamed herself for not believing in me and my dreams. My sisters would have one less brother that they would never see again.

As for me, I would have been on the other side alone and in darkness. I was happy that God stepped in and changed my mind. Lord, you are the one who did the miracle and I thank you for everything. I also thank you for the plans that you have for me (**Jeremiah 29: 11**):

> *"For I know the plans I have for you, declares the LORD, plans to prosper you and not to harm you, plans to give you hope and a future."*

The middle of the school year was fast approaching so I had to work hard in the weight room. I also had to work extra hard in the classroom because wrestling season was about to begin. The bullies had not gone away either and I felt as if the whole world was working against me.

My friends could not protect me from the bullies. The bullies' tactics were getting more brutal and I was trying to be strong, but they outnumbered me. They moved from cursing me out to blatant attempts to fight me.

I said to God, "God, why me? Why do I have to be bullied and thrown into trash cans?" I was tired of being bullied, but the Word of God in **Isaiah 41:10, 13** was my comfort:

> *"Fear thou not; for I am with thee: be not dismayed; for I am thy God: I will strengthen thee; yea: I will help thee; yea; I will uphold thee with the right hand of my righteousness.* [13]*For I the God thy God will hold thy right hand, saying unto thee, fear not; I will help thee."*

Wrestling in the 9th Grade

When wrestling season began, everyone on the team thought that I was going to lose, but I said to myself, *PDIG (People Doubt, I Grind)*. My belief was that *if I was born poor it was not my fault, but if I die poor, that will be my fault.* Therefore, I cannot stop grinding for my dreams.

One day, at the wrestling practice, they said to me, "You must work three times as hard as everyone else because you are an African American. You are considered disabled and you have to work hard anyway."

I continued weight training after schools. My Mom cooked food for the family and everyone thanked her for her hard work. We would pray over the food and I always prayed for my Mom and Dad. My father may not have been with us, but he was supporting the family the best he could.

My Freshman Year and the ESPN Documentation

After doing my homework, I would train in the gym to strengthen my arms. I trained for three days straight and never forgot to study. In the State Wrestling match, I ended up placing third at 106 lbs. with a record of 51-10 at the High School in Jackson. By the end of my freshmen year, I had ESPN following me during spring training.

ESPN documented my training sessions and asked me questions. They wanted to know about my passion for doing all of the things that I did. I told them that I just wanted to play sports and end discrimination. I told them that I loved playing football and that a lot of coaches tried to stop my advancement in the sport. I told them that in spite of my disability, I have the ability that God gave me.

The ESPN was watching my advancement because they wanted to tell my story, but I just kept doing what was in my heart, which was to be best that I could be. I have a genuine love for sports. I chose to stay humble because I know that just as God picks a person up, He can knock the person back down to erase pride.

Football training was going very well and the coaches began to push me hard, but I loved all of the spring trainings because I got to train with different national teams. After ESPN had collected a lot of footage from my training sessions, they wished me the best in my future and were happy for me.

We eventually moved back to Henry County. The spring training was over and I waited for another New Year so I could start the 10th grade.

My Big Brother is a High Graduate

By the end of my freshmen year, my brother graduated from high school. We congratulated him and had a graduation party. My big brother was now a high school graduate and I knew that I had to be one too.

I had to do what my big brother did because he set an example for me. We brought him some gifts and cake as he blew out the candles. He was the first high school graduate among my siblings. We all had to graduate like our big brother.

Chapter 15: Life in the 10th Grade

Another Change of School

The summer ended and I was glad to know that I was heading into my sophomore year of high school. We had a great summer, but it was time to get back to learning.

When school began, we enrolled at the High School in Henry County. My mindset was that the students were most likely going to hate me, so I was prepared for another year of football and fighting, but my sophomore year turned out to be briefly refreshing. I met my teachers and tried to get to know them. They were very good teachers and I never had an attitude with any of them. I got used to their homework, tests and pop quizzes without any problem.

The high school coach was named Starr. After trying out for the team, I was accepted. On my very first day of practice, I had on the school gear from head to toe. Everyone had their eyes on me and my heart was pounding very fast because I was super excited. I lowered my head down as the coach told everyone about me joining the team. As usual, they all doubted my ability to play the game.

They asked, "Who is this?" I said, "I am Devon Berry. I have played on a lot of teams and I have tons of experience. I am very good at getting tackles and stopping any runners." When they heard this, they said, "We have to see your talent in a game." I told them that I will prove myself in a game and bring a win to the team.

Overcoming Another Mean Coach in My Sophomore Year

The first couple of months went by very smoothly. I was very cool with everyone and they called me 'the Berry'. I believe that the only disability in life is a bad attitude. I was doing very well on the team until the day my coach decided to not let me participate in practice. I got an attitude and threw a huge temper tantrum while insisting that I must play. At this point, the other players began to laugh because I was different.

The coach said, "We don't want you on the field. F...k you! You are nothing but scum. We need better players than people with disabilities. You have to choose another sport that matches your condition." I was very angry at what he said because I love to play football. The other players jumped on the coach's bandwagon saying, "We don't need losers like you. We've seen better players that can at least walk."

Although they hurt my feelings with their words, I stayed with the team and begged the coach to at least let me practice. I told him I did not care if it was just one play at practice, but he should let me in. As I begged him, he replied, "One thing that I don't like about you is that you think that this is your team and that you are above the law. What are you going to do if I put you out there on the field?" I said, "I am going to practice like everyone else. I just want to feel like I'm a part of the team."

He said, "Ok, we will see." The very next day, the football players that were in my class began to pick on me more than before. I remember that the Lesson was on World History and we were starting to learn about the Civil War.

The teacher wrote an assignment on the board telling us to read about the Civil War and write an essay on it. I started reviewing the Civil War lesson so I could start writing my essay.

I learned that the Civil War was about the North and the South fighting over slavery. The South wanted to keep the blacks as slaves and continued to make money off of them. The North hated slavery and wanted it ended. The Civil War lasted for a couple of years and the North won the battle. I kept writing for a while before heading to the next football practice. The players were still picking on me, but I still stayed on the field and trained with them. As we were going to the locker room, they started bullying me.

Also, they had started stealing my equipment from my locker and the coach tried playing me without the missing equipment. They were so evil to me. I tried to explain to the coach about the bullying and missing equipment, but he did not listen. I eventually found my equipment and made it to football training. They did everything in the book to make me look bad, but that did not stop me. They did not stop their evil acts against me, but I always gave 110% on the field.

The coach still treated me badly and my teachers still doubted me, but I stayed focused. I always tried to do my best with my homework and quizzes. They had their ways of looking at me, but I never yelled at those teachers because I knew that I was destined for greatness. They could not take it away.

I was breaking barriers because I was strong and no longer weak. I was very aware that He who dwelt within me, the Holy Ghost, made me a conqueror. Therefore, I never ceased to praise and lift up His Holy Name.

Evicted Again and Living in a Hotel

Everything was going well in school, but bad things began to happen at home. We eventually got evicted from our house and we had nowhere to go. After looking for someone to live with, we began staying with my Auntie for a while. We were going to school with no place to call home. As for me, I decided to work harder because I was blessed to be living with my Auntie.

The football players did not care about my personal problems. Instead, they kept on talking about me and making me feel worse. My teacher handed me more homework and I had to finish all my homework before football training. This was very hard and I was praying daily because I was suffering spiritually and physically. All these things hit me at the same time.

We were eventually put out of our Auntie's house and we stayed in a hotel for two long years. My sisters, my Mom and I were forced to stay in one room. In the mornings, my Mom would drop us off at school before going to work. We worked hard to pass our classes to ease her burdens. The room was a little small at times, but we counted our blessings because we could have been on the street.

At this time, my big brother John was in the Navy and doing very well. We kept him in our prayers and he kept us in his prayers while fighting for our freedom and protection. We were glad that John was fighting to keep this country safe from terrorists.

I was having a hard time with all my activities and everyone doubted my abilities. I wanted to cry because I felt hopeless.

Mom Remarried

While still living in a one room at the hotel, my Mom married Bobby Amis. That being said, we all had it 'rough' staying in one room with two adults and three grown children. We had to make a lot of sacrifices with the beds and someone had to sleep on the floor or couch. I was usually on the couch with the foldable bed.

I was drowning in my sorrow because I wanted to live in a better place than this. I was tired of being crowded in one room with no room of my own. In the winter, the room was very hot at times while the outside was cold. As a result, we had to put up with the heat or go outside in the freezing air.

I was truly happy that my brother was not with us at that time because it was a complete mess. My brother sometimes called me to ask about the family and would I tell him about our living condition. Meanwhile, we continued with school and Mom with her job. In class, the teacher handed out the test consisting of 55 questions, but I was ready after two weeks of studying.

After the test, I prepared for my football training because we were having a game. We all got into our uniforms and went to the field. The coaches chose the players and I was not picked, so I watched as both sides were nearing a tie. They finally called my name and put me in the game.

My teammates told me to hold the line or we would lose so I was determined to hold the line. The other team's quarterback aimed the ball at their player and the player was running in front when I suddenly tackled him. My team scored a touchdown. The other team never saw it coming. We won the game, but no one gave me any credit.

No Shopping for New Things for 5 Straight Years

At the hotel, I began thinking about all the times we had moved and suffered without going shopping for five straight years. Having nothing and struggling from day to day humbled my family. We constantly prayed that God would make a way out of no way for us. We went from not knowing where we were going to live to not having clean underwear for six straight months!

Although we were having a hard time, we still gave God the glory. The school year was passing by fast and I was worried about my tests because my teachers were giving them frequently. Most nights while everyone was sleeping, I studied for an extra three hours.

The football team was having another game, but I was not playing in the game. Again, the coach refused to put me in the game. I was a benchwarmer and I hated just sitting there. My team was winning and I wanted to play too. My ambition was to win but, with no hope except a dream and a vision, I held my head high knowing that God never lies and was with me. I was angry because Coach never put me in the game and my family wanted to see me play.

The next morning, I went to each of my classes, took my tests and headed home. The school year was over. In the hotel room, we talked about our next year since we would be high school juniors. The days passed by fast and we were three weeks from a new school year.

During our time off school, we walked around the hotel because of boredom; we needed something to do. My brother returned and told us interesting stories about his experiences in the Navy.

My Dream to Be Understood and Respected

I had a dream of me giving a speech at my school and the people finally looked at me with respect and understood my struggles. In the speech, I told them that I had struggled with being bullied in school, teachers doubting me and keeping me down and teammates that hated me and did not want to be on the same field with me.

I assured them that the struggles did not stop me, but made me stronger. As a matter of fact, they helped to open my eyes to the big picture concerning my life. I knew that the picture would never be perfect, but I would always be Devon Berry and no one could change me.

I told them that I would rather be my true self than to keep faking my happiness. I informed them that the school brought me some sorrow and joy, but that I would never change any of the events that happened because they helped to shape me. I stated that my struggles and pains were cured by God and God had never turned His back on me or my family. As a result, we would always worship God.

When I was done with my speech, everyone began cheering for me and they were shouting my name. The dream ended, I woke up and began watching TV.

We Transferred to a High School in Henry County

By the end of my 10th grade year, my sisters and I decided to go to the new school in Henry County. After a three-month delay, we moved to our new high school and were so happy to start our studies.

On the first very day, I met a man named Bruce Johnson. He was of medium height with blonde hair and brown eyes. He was the Video and Broadcast teacher and always talked to me about Jesus Christ. Although the seed of the Word of God was already planted in me, he always talked to me about Christ and His wonders around the world. He said to me, "You just have to believe in Him and when you do, anything is possible." He and my mentor Bill Renji, who was also in a wheelchair, talked a lot about Christ to me.

Bill Renji was a Caucasian with brown eyes. Before this, I was blinded to the fact that Christ was the answer that I had been asking God for. I needed to know Him more.

They continued to minister to me about Christ and, with the help of my mother and sisters, I got to know Christ more. As a result, I began to build a stronger relationship with him.

The wrestling season was about to begin and the coach was named Morton. I talked to him about how I placed sixth in state wrestling at 113 lbs. in my sophomore year. He seemed to be cool at the time but, eventually, he did not like me. He purposely put bigger students in my weight class to beat me. I thought Coach Morton was different from the other coaches, but he was just like them. Other than that, I enjoyed my new school.

ESPN Came Back and the Coach Was Not Happy

The weight training coach was also the football coach. His name was Coach Ashley. He was muscular and did not like me at all. We did not get along and, one day, he threw me out the weight room. Therefore, I needed to show him some respect, because I was playing on the football team.

Within two weeks of my waiting, spring training rolled around and ESPN returned. Coach Ashley said, "ESPN ain't following me." He continued to yell and scream about how I would not compete. He said, "How dare I put you out there on the field. They (ESPN) are here for real players. This school has hundreds of better players than you. You need to stop dreaming in this world."

He talked about how unfit I was, but I told myself that I would not be stopped. ESPN had come to the school to follow me and it was great!

From the Hotel to a House and Eviction Again

With all these things going on, I never lost focus on our home situation. Knowing that we were homeless with no help, made me more determined to have no excuses. We eventually found a home and moved out of the hotel.

We were so happy to be back in a home and to have a place to call home. I was doing better in my classes because God had blessed all of us with our own room, but the good times did not last long.

We had only lived in the home for a couple of months before we were evicted again. We moved back to the apartment and the times were getting very hard but, through it all, God kept us.

Playing a New Wheelchair Sport — Basketball!

I began playing the Wheelchair Sports basketball and the team was called the Alligators. The coach was Harlem Matthews and he allowed me to play on the team. We were in the center of the field when the Alligators got the ball and, as we were moving towards the hoop, they took the ball and rolled to the basket. We were trying to block their shot by rolling in front of them. They missed their first shot and we caught the ball again.

I began rolling the ball and we scored the point. The game went for another 40 minutes and the Alligators won. I was very happy to be on a winning team. At that time, I was playing football, wrestling and playing the wheelchair sports - all at the same time! Coach Ashley still did not like me and one of the reasons was because I was not showing up for the workouts. I explained to him that I could not show up all the time because I didn't have a ride.

I can remember sitting in the cold locker room because he had kicked me out. I suffered in the cold locker room while everyone else was playing on the field. Coach Ashley continued to be cruel to me and even hated that I was in the locker room. I told my Mom about it and how he tried to kick me off the team because I was not showing up for workouts. My Mom told me not to give up even though times were hard, so I continued to give God the glory.

I had three long tests the next morning after my conversation with my Mom so I studied. The next day, I went into class and started the first test. Everyone thought I was going to fail because of my situation, but I passed that test, scoring a 90! The students were surprised about my grade.

I went to my next class and took the next test. I had studied very hard for these tests and I refused to fail. I took the third test and I was very calm through it all. I was blessed to pass all three.

Balancing Academics with Sports

When the class bell rung, I was back at the wheelchair sports. My teammates were the same students from the last time. We moved to the middle of the court and they tossed the ball in the air. I caught the ball and I began rolling to the basket to toss the ball in. When I did, we scored our first point.

Next, the other team got the ball and they scored a three pointer. As a result, the Alligators needed to try a lot harder. In the end, we beat the other team by five points! I loved playing the game, but I had to return to the hotel to study and prepare for an upcoming wrestling match. This was the most challenging year for me because I had too much homework and too many other sports to play.

After class, I got ready for my wrestling match. I had been training for this match because I lost the last round in the previous one. When my opponent came into the ring, I was not afraid of him. We met in the middle of the ring and the coach walked over to check us out. We were both ready to wrestle.

My opponent tried to get me in a chokehold, but I stopped his advance by holding his feet. He then tried to break the hold, but it was no good and I won the rematch! We shook each other's hand.

The coach was surprised to see my victory over my opponent and he began to respect me a little. That night, I had a dream about the coach letting me play in the games in order to prove myself to the team. In the dream, they had been disrespecting me and I needed to gain their respect. The dream ended and that day at the field games, I was ready for the game. I went to my class, turned in my work, took the pop quiz and set my mind on the football game.

I walked into the locker room and got into my uniform. We went to the field where the crowd was already cheering. We had fun in the first quarter and it was a good start because we immediately scored a touchdown and everyone was shouting. In the fourth quarter, the game was tied.

The coach called my name and people began cheering for me. I moved to my position and waited on the play. When the quarterback hiked the ball, I looked for the runner. The runner was coming very fast and I tackled him with all my might to get the ball. We ran with the ball to the other side and our runner scored a touchdown. We won the game and everyone cheered for our team. My family was cheering for me and they made the loudest screams.

After the game, I headed to the hotel where we were living again, but I felt like a winner. My Mom ordered some pizza to celebrate our victory. It was at this time that I realized I was almost a senior and that school would soon be over. I got into my bed dreaming about my senior year and I was very happy.

Chapter 16: My Final Year of High School

My Desire to Finish High School with Good Memories

My senior year finally began and the football season was around the corner. I made the decision to get to know all my teachers and the Principal because I wanted to leave high school with some good memories.

In the very first class period, the teacher was happy to see the seniors and she wanted all of us to graduate at the end of the year. Each student stood up and talked about themselves. I talked about the struggles of being picked on and about the fact that no one cared about me. I told them about how the world kept telling me to give up my dreams, but I refused and how I would not be with them right then without my faith.

I let them know that I believed in God and that He can do all types of wonders. I stated that I would continue to trust Him to direct my paths, as stated in **Proverbs 3:5-6**:

> *"Trust in the LORD with all thine heart; and lean not unto thine own understanding. 6 In all thy ways acknowledge him, and he shall direct thy paths."*

My teacher handed everyone some notes to study in preparation for the quiz scheduled on the next day. She was a very nice teacher and the year started off right and the football games were great. We played some of the tops schools and beat them. Many people came for the last game because they wanted see the players and they did not care if we won or loss.

My last high school football game was surreal. We played against Pike County. The first three quarters were very fast paced, and some of the players were getting injured, but they kept on playing. I did not play the whole game, but the coach finally called my name and number and I got on the field with only 40 minutes left.

The crowd began to scream *62, 62, 62,* which was my number. As I was waiting in my position, the crowd was going nuts and calling my name. I tackled the player from the ankles and helped cause a fumble. *Even I was in awe!* I was in complete shock as I asked myself, "Did I do that?"

I said to the coach, "You should put me in more." He said, "You are probably right." As for me, I refused to let my different ability determine who I was. I was going to find a way to be successful because I believed what God's Word said in **Psalm 100:5**:

> *"For the LORD is good; his mercy is everlasting; and his truth endureth to all generations."*

And also **Psalm 23:4:**

> *"Yea, though I walk through the valley of the shadow of death, I will fear no evil: for thou art with me; thy rod and thy staff they comfort me."*

My Story on Several Nation News Outlets

We played a Division 2 National Championship and after a game at one of the high schools in Sandy Creek, I took a picture with the kicker Benjamin Rutland. (The picture ended up getting 26 thousand likes and 11 thousand shares on Facebook. It was only the beginning of God's blessing in my life, because I had rededicated my life to Christ the week before the game.)

I remembered how everyone started taking me seriously after my story was covered on the news channels. My story ended up in the national news media from coast to coast and, on November 1, 2015, I was the Honor Captain for the Atlanta Falcons! It was covered by the Atlanta Journal, Constitution, Channel 11, Channel 2, Fox 5 and many other news media. I was interviewed by Ryan Cameron on the morning of November 11, 2015.

I Got a Wrestling Scholarship

I landed a wrestling scholarship to St. Cloud State University in Minnesota! I was the first student to ever sign a scholarship at the High School in Hampton, GA. My story was featured on ESPN on December 15, 2015. My high school wrestling career record was 150 wins to 39 losses, qualifying me for the 2016 Paralympic tryouts which take place in 2020.

I sometimes wished my brother was with me to see what God was doing in my life, but I told him all about it and how much I missed him. My Mom was happy for all of my blessings because she was the one that kept encouraging me to keep the faith.

My Last Goal in High School

I was blessed a lot during my last year of high school. My last goal was to pass all of my classes and make my mother proud. The students treated me a lot better; the coaches that hated me became nicer. Many people were now looking up to me and wanted to be my friend. My teachers finally stopped doubting me as they witnessed my successes.

In class, the teacher handed out some homework and midterm study sheets. I went home to 'grind'. I finished all my homework, including showing the steps I took arrive at the answers.

The midterms were six weeks away and the study packets came in very handy because they helped me to focus on the assigned materials. The next six weeks went by fast. I took the Math, English and Science midterm exams. Although they were lengthy and difficult, I had studied hard. I focused and took my time completing them.

Having given the exams my best shot, I was very tired when school was over and my Mom came to take me back to the hotel. My Mom took us out to eat because she was very proud of us.

Final Exams

We have been through a lot struggles, suffering and changing homes. We were almost on the street several times, but God blessed us again with this last place to stay and we have not lost it.

The next tests were the finals. Again, I studied hard and focused during the exams. The grades were to be posted a week later. My science teacher loved all of the students and wished us all the best of luck as she handed out the final exams. (I loved science because of the experiments and theories.)

I prayed over the test because I was nervous. I opened the test and looked at the questions as I began to answer them. There were a lot of words that looked similar, but meant different things.

I wrote down my answers and turned in my paper. The last final was English and I also gave it my best. The teacher told us that she was going to miss us all and wanted us to never forget the memory of high school, a once in a lifetime event. After the finals were over, the students were free to go.

Graduation from High School

Although I still I had to deal with all kinds of people in my senior year, I made it to graduation. This was one of the proudest moments of my life because I knew that the struggles were finally over. No one could stop my blessing and my dream.

At the end, my coaches looked at me and they smiled at my progress, but I knew that they failed in their attempts to bring me down. My family and I went back to the hotel and I called my brother. He was very proud of me because I stood up to the bullies and the coaches. We all had a group prayer before my brother signed off and headed back to his Navy duties.

My family and I told God that we were very thankful for His help in our education and for protecting us from all evil. We all knew that we would be no where without Him. We all need to know and remember that God is real and He cares about us.

The teacher also told us that Prom was a once in a lifetime event, so everyone was preparing for graduations and Prom parties. We had been together for the whole year and we had so many memories: the sad times of fighting in the hallways and classrooms as well as the good times of coming together and planning events. There were also the bad times of cursing out the teachers for no reason, but we will always be known as the best class of Hampton High School. We knew that we would be remembered by our teachers and I prayed for them all.

The graduation ceremony was coming up and they mailed the tickets. The ceremony was scheduled at the high school on the football field. I walked to the stage with my sisters and we were official high school graduates! No one can ever take it away from us and we took some pictures with our family members. We have a very big family, but only a handful could come to the event.

My father came to support his children and we took a picture of the family with him. This was the best of all my memories and my Mom was very proud of us. She was so happy to have three graduates in the same month.

As for me, I knew that I was going to miss all of my fellow seniors because, through it all, my high school years were fun and I had a message to tell the whole world. I want the world to know that Devon Berry is not intimidated and he is no quitter.

Future Goal in Life

The next step in my life after graduation was to plan the next phase of my future. My plan was to go to college and major in Mass Communications so that I could become a Sports Broadcaster.

I aspire to work for ESPN someday, but my immediate plan is to get a Bachelor's degree. I also want to be part of the 2020 Tryout for the Paralympics in Track and Field as well as continue as a Public Speaker and an Author who inspires people. I want to continue shining my light and doing the will of GOD but, most importantly, stand up for Christ Jesus. My reason for this desire is because I believe Dr. Martin Luther King Jr.'s words:

"Darkness cannot drive out darkness; only light can do that. Hate cannot drive out hate; only love can do that".

Therefore, it is my belief that, "Sin cannot drive out sin; only Jesus Christ can do that. Hate cannot drive out hate; only the love of Jesus Christ can do that. Darkness cannot outshine darkness; only the light of Jesus Christ can do that." Everyone talks about black lives matter, white lives matter and how all lives matter. The only thing that matters is, "Is your soul saved?" Are you sanctified and filled with the Holy Spirit? At the end, only those who brought forth good fruits will matter. This is why we are told the following in **Matthew 3:8-11:**

"Bring forth therefore fruits meet for repentance: 9 And think not to say within yourselves, We have Abraham to our father: for I say unto you, that God is able of these stones to raise up children unto Abraham. 10 And now also the axe is laid unto the root of the trees: therefore every tree which bringeth not forth good fruit is hewn down, and cast into the fire. 11 I indeed baptize you with water unto repentance: but he that

cometh after me is mightier than I, whose shoes I am not worthy to bear: he shall baptize you with the Holy Ghost, and with fire:"

The Lord Jesus Christ died to save the world so will you be ready when He comes? Get your life right with Jesus Christ because He only wants one thing — the pure in heart! Enter into His gates with thanksgiving and into His courts with praise. Be thankful and bless His name. I will like to leave with you with these questions:

- Will your work of iniquity or your 'good work' be enough when you stand before Jesus Christ on that Great Day?

- Will you be able to stand and receive the Crown of Life?

Conclusion

How to Dedicate Your Life to Jesus

Now that you have read this book, my message to you is that in order for you to be successful, you must face your fears and let God direct your paths. I advise you to get to know the Lord Jesus Christ by asking Him to come into your life and be your Savior. He saved me and countless others. He will save you too because He is the same yesterday, today and forever. He will deliver you and set you free from the bondage in your life. Below is a prayer that will help you to invite Him into your life.

> *"Lord Jesus, I believe that You are the Son of God and that because of my sins, You suffered, died on the Cross and was buried. On the third day, God the Father raised You from the dead. Of my own free-will, I invite You today to come into my life today and be my Lord. Forgive me of all my sins, cleanse me with You blood and give me eternal life. I confess you as my Lord from this day on."*

God can help you no matter what your situation is. Do not throw in the towel. The Word of God instructs us that our faith should not stand in the wisdom of men, but in the power of God (**1 Corinthians 2:5**). In **Matthew 6:9-13**, the Lord Jesus instructed us on how to pray:

> *"After this manner therefore pray ye: Our Father which art in heaven, Hallowed be thy name. 10 Thy kingdom come. Thy will be done in earth, as it is in heaven. 11 Give us this day our daily bread. 12 And forgive us our debts, as we forgive our debtors. 13 And lead us not into temptation, but deliver us from evil: For thine is the kingdom, and the power, and the glory, forever. Amen."*

To contact Devon Berry:

TheDevonBerryStory.org

or

TheDevonBerryStory@Gmail.com

Also, please leave a review on Amazon.com and help spread the word by telling others about this book.

May God bless you always and remember that there are no excuses!

-The Devon Berry Story

31787549R00086

Made in the USA
San Bernardino, CA
07 April 2019